Anthology House

ANTHOLOGY HOUSE

A Visionary Ecology Project

ASEI Arts

ASEI Arts, a division of Light Vibe LLC
New York

Anthology House Copyright © 2018 by ASEI Arts, a division of Light Vibe LLC. All Rights Reserved.

CONTENTS

Anthology House	vii
ASEI Arts	ix
Dedication	xi
Foreword	xiii
Ann Malaspina United States	1
To Safety	3
Ndaba Sibanda Zimbabwe	5
From City to Rusticity	7
Fish Fizzling Out	9
Cultural Centre	11
Marguerite Harrold United States	13
Astral Projection	15
Chicago March 22	17
Anne Ipsen United States	19
Green Valley a novel excerpt	21
Chapter 1: Journey to Xanadu	21
Chapter 2: The Williams Hill CSA	34
Chapter 3: Doc Reed and Nurse Molly	44
Brian Burt United States	53
Storm Rider a short story	55
C.E. Wagner United States	71

Repurpose   73
a novel excerpt

Chapter 1: Wesley   73

Chapter 2: Nora   83

Chapter 3: Wesley   91

Chapter 4: Nora   96

Chapter 5: Wesley   102

Colin Waterman   111
United Kingdom

The Hesperian Dilemma   113
a novel excerpt

Devanshi Jackson   133
India & United States

Reasoner   135
a short story

Elizabeth Esguerra Castillo   137
Philippines

Take Me Back to Genesis   139

Eyes without a Face   141

Maia Kumari Gilman   143
Canada & United States

Bioreme   145
a short story

ANTHOLOGY
HOUSE

A collection curated by Maia Kumari Gilman
Edited by Jillian Magalaner Stone
2018
ASEI Arts, a division of Light Vibe LLC
New York City

ASEI ARTS

Copyright ©2018 ASEI Arts

This is a collection of works of fiction and poetry. Names, characters, places, company names and incidents are fictionalized products of the authors' imaginations or are used fictitiously and are not to be construed as real. Any resemblance to actual events, locales, organizations, or persons, living or dead, is entirely coincidental. All rights reserved. No part of this book may be used or reproduced in any manner whatsoever without written permission from the publisher except in the case of brief quotations embodied in critical articles or reviews.

ASEI Arts, a division of Light Vibe LLC, 112 West 27th Street, Suite 500, New York NY 10001
email: admin@aseiarts.com
Published by ASEI Arts, a division of Light Vibe LLC, New York NY
Distributed by Ingram
Title: *Anthology House: A Visionary Ecology Project*
Maia Kumari Gilman, curator
Jillian Magalaner Stone, editor
Description: First International Edition
New York NY: ASEI Arts, a division of Light Vibe LLC, 2018
Identifiers:
ISBN 978-0-9988421-6-5 Paperback
ISBN 978-0-9988421-5-8 Ebook
First International Edition 2018
Designer: Lori Dalvi
www.aseiarts.com

DEDICATION

To the winds who carry our voices

FOREWORD

This project came into being during and after Hurricanes Harvey, Irma, and Maria, which affected the southern United States and Caribbean nations in the summer of 2017. As someone who experienced Hurricanes Irene and Sandy in New Jersey and New York in 2011 and 2012, I felt the impact of storms on one's day-to-day well-being and was inspired to create my own personal way to reach those newly affected.

My way of reaching out, no matter the topic, is through the creative arts, whether in written or visual form. I'd previously written a visionary ecology novel and published it through my company, ASEI Arts, a division of Light Vibe LLC (formerly a company exclusively dedicated to Reiki healing arts services, later repurposed into a general outreach of creative and healing arts). I had so much fun with that project, my eco-fiction novel *The Erenwine Agenda,* that it seemed only natural to invite others to join the party. But what would be the basis of the event? Surely not a hurricane.

The storms came while I was at the Appalachian Mountain Club's Highland Center in New Hampshire, the same place I was inspired to write my own novel and to incorporate the rewriting of storms. It seemed easy to pick up the phone to call Habitat for Humanity in Texas and offer this idea of sharing an anthology of writing in the form of a fundraiser. All the profits from the anthology would go to hurricane relief in the South. The people I spoke to were busy with their own work and yet very appreciative of the efforts we would offer, through ASEI Arts, and said they'd be happy to receive the profits from the project for hurricane relief. Later in the fall, Habitat for Humanity created Habitat Hammers Back, an initiative to offer relief specifically to those areas hit by the hurricanes of the summer of 2017.

Once I put out the call for submissions, I realized the magnitude of the undertaking: the first submissions came from an author in Africa. How could I incorporate the writings of an African author into an anthology that is focused on North America? He was writing about the plight of various local cultures in relation to the ecological changes taking place on that continent, and yet he was happy to contribute his writing to this project. Was it relevant? How could I address his concerns while focused on those of the Habitat Hammers Back initiative, which by every measure was local to the Americas? I meditated on it and realized the opportunity: of course we are global. Of course we are connected. This year the anthology will benefit the Americas. In another year, we can make an anthology to benefit African nations, and so on. It is an ongoing and intertwined project.

After I'd come to that realization, the next pieces fell into place. Was the next author's work too angst-ridden? And if so, why was that a problem? Visionary ecology spans the entire spectrum of experience and reaction. Of course there is angst. And of course there is relief from it. Relief was the stated focus for the anthology, and every writer who submitted work touched on the idea of relief in some way, just not how I would personally approach it. The trajectory of work from the ancestral to that of the future, evidenced here in this anthology, represents a large body of thought that extends well beyond my own perspective.

While I tend toward the bright and shiny, others have a more dystopian view of the future. I think the range is rich and reflects the diversity of opinion about our common future.

Was religion part of it? Not for me, and I'd stated that in the call for submissions. But then, our submissions call was bookended by another challenger to my guidelines: a writer from the Philippines who flows with the spirit of her own divinity. Her work touched me while simultaneously challenging my notion of "let's keep this spiritual but not religious." Why not let religion flow into it? It is part of the perspective of one author. And so, the work is included.

This all begs the question, what is visionary ecology? Here is my summation: it is a collaborative envisioning of the opportunity of our shared domain. It challenges assumptions about rightness and alignment in our lives and work, and wraps to include all perspectives, no matter where they are on the spectrum of religion, identity, or politics. Does religion play a role? For sure. But this is not a religious anthology, and I am not exploring a religious view of a visionary ecology. Each individual may come to their own terms with these larger questions of universal manifestation. And yet, these questions of origins, journeys, and destinations do persist and provoke.

Are we well at our core? I believe we are. I believe we have a tendency to wellness and that when we shine a light, whether on individuals or on communities, we brighten the path for others and amplify the wellness of our shared environments.

I hope you will enjoy, be provoked, and in turn pick up a pen to write your own view of the future.

Blessings,

Maia Kumari Gilman

ANN MALASPINA

United States

Born in Brooklyn NY, Ann Malaspina is an award-winning children's author and poet who often writes about the environment and social justice. She has an MFA in Writing from Vermont College of Fine Arts. When she's not out looking for the tiny endangered bog turtle for her next project, she writes under a skylight in Northern New Jersey. Her picture book *A Scarf For Keiko* is coming out in 2019.

TO SAFETY

The salamanders march like soldiers
in camouflage green, carrying

their lives on long slender backs
and slippery tails, defying all peril

on a road in the rain. Not one of us
would dare to make the journey.

Arms raised, we line up like peaceniks,
shielding them from tires and hooves,

falling objects, beaks, and boots,
saving the world one salamander at a time.

NDABA SIBANDA

Zimbabwe

Recipient of a Starry Night ART School Scholarship in 2015, Ndaba Sibanda has contributed to more than thirty anthologies, including *Its Time, Poems For Haiti- a South African Anthology, Snippets, Voices For Peace, New Shoots, Seeing Beyond the Surface Volume II, Black Communion, Resurrection of a Sunflower* (edited by Catfish McDaris and Dr. Marc Pietrzykowski), and *Eternal Snow: A Worldwide Anthology of One Hundred Twenty Five Poetic Intersections with Himalayan Poet Yuyutsu RD Sharma* (Nirala Publications, 2017). Sibanda is the author of *Love O'clock, The Dead Must Be Sobbing, Of the Saliva and the Tongue, Cutting-edge Cache: Unsympathetic Untruth,* and *Football of Fools.* He also edited *Free Fall.* Sibanda`s forthcoming poetry anthology is *As If They Minded* (Pski's Porch Publishing).

FROM CITY TO RUSTICITY

They sought to escape
the distractions of a busy life,
the bustles and hustles of the city;
Then they packed their bags, off they
went with their wandering cats and dogs
to the remotest of villages where they hoped
to become farmers of simplicity and tranquility.

FISH FIZZLING OUT

What the fish
Could not do with force
It did with stashed funds
Now cashlessness and coldness coo

The fallouts and factions are fierce
From fawning to fiends the tables turned
Today they sing the downtrodden's familiar tune
Yesterday's oppressor's hard-hearted keepers!

Elders say what is endless is ominous
Fact is fattening even fools are fed up
The fish is running short of water
Fishy final throw of the dice

Every flying bird-sly and sleek-
Ultimately lands somewhere somehow
For time is a trial to those who disrespect
And destroy its hand and its sanctity and humanity

CULTURAL CENTRE

It was a weekend of inspiration and revival
The Centre took away my nagging nakedness
And clothed me with the charms of tradition

The charms of tradition echoed in their spaces
They exuded an African grandeur second to none
I felt the deepest desire to be myself and my mirror

MARGUERITE HARROLD

United States

Marguerite Harrold holds a Master of Fine Arts in Poetry (with Honors) from Columbia College Chicago, is a member of the Community of Writers at Squaw Valley, and has attended the Bread Loaf Orion Environmental Writers' Conference. Harrold recently retired from the Chicago Department of Public Health after twenty years in the Divisions of HIV Prevention and Environmental Health in order to pursue poetry and naturalist work while also traveling the world. In 2016 Harrold earned naturalist certifications in Interpretation and in Conservation and Land Management from The Morton Arboretum . She also holds a Controlled Burn Certification from Chicago Wilderness.

Harrold's poetry has been or will be published in the following journals: *Rigorous, SHANTIH, Tipton Poetry Journal, Black Napkin Press, Oculus Vox, Poetry City U.S.A, Wimperbang!, Melbourne Poetry Project, RHINO: The Poetry Forum, Spaces Between Us: Poetry, Prose and Art on HIV/AIDS, Eleven Eleven: Journal of Literature & Art, Criminal Class Review, Squaw Valley Review,* and *Columbia Poetry Review.*

Harrold currently lives on the road and expects to be in Fiji by Fall 2018.

ASTRAL PROJECTION

Email even more distant
Than the miles between us
There are no mountains in it

No hollers where the crick meets its echo
No spaces for breath to unite under a common hum
No pauses filled with answers

I never got to voice
My preferred method
Of communication

Uninvited
Just as you predicted
You heard me in the wind and rain

Tropical storms swirling your locks into wetlands
On your birthday
Winds that bend the knees of cypress trees

I wished for this for me
Sky split into three
Adventure in all that chaos

Longing
Luxuriated in the smell of mourning
And mold and Spanish moss

Splinters from a Shotgun's porch stinging my thigh
Solace in the spirit's questions
Snakes swimming figure 8s around my ankles

For you
I wanted only
Sun showers and magic

I suspect you're sweating onto someone else's skin
And then another's
And another's

I hope you dream of my wetness in your eyes
Dripping from your chin
Splashing the curve of your hips in those boxers

When you duck out onto the porch
And see the crow that wakes you up every morning
You believe me now

They really do mimic human vocalizations
In New Orleans they actually caw lagniappe
And this time you'll swear it was me

CHICAGO MARCH 22

Spring here is grey and brown
Still groggy & half asleep
Groaning and scratching herself
She is the dirty faced cousin of Fall

Mud matted in her hair
Green roots not yet grown in
She wakes and wrestles with Winter
Her crush so deep she's reluctant to let him go

She begs him for snow
Two months past his lease
Anxious to feel his icy fingers flirting
Flipping white lace jewels into the air
His behemoth breath up her skirt
And down again freezing things in place

They meet in the evening stillness
Melting into a messy embrace
Of soot and slush and smashed up dog shit

She knows her time is short
Slinging sleet as she rinses everything that rises

She's late
She knows

Summer her sassy sister
Is always early
And impatient
As are we

ANNE IPSEN

United States

Writer, speaker, and environmentalist Anne Ipsen has written two memoirs and five novels. Her novels *At the Concord of the Rivers* and *Abigail's Legacy* reflect her interest in history and love of the town of Concord. Ipsen has recently turned to the environment and the looming issue of climate change. *Green Valley: a climate change novel* takes place in the near future in a rural community that models a sustainable way of life as New England leads the Carbon Revolution. Together with the historical "Concord" books, this cli-fi novel forms a multigenerational trilogy that spans 350 years of Massachusetts history. Ipsen is currently working on an environmental workbook intended primarily for faith communities, with a projected publication date of 2018.

Before leaving academia to write full time, Dr. Ipsen was Professor of Public Health at the University of Minnesota. She and her husband now live in Cambridge, Massachusetts. They have three children and five grandchildren.

GREEN VALLEY

a novel excerpt

Chapter 1: Journey to Xanadu

Wednesday, June 15, 2022

It's finished. I really have done it—dragged Bill away from the only life he's ever known. Will I regret the decision to leave NY and all that implies? Possibly, but right now I'm only relieved that I've closed that door behind us. By starting this journal, I seal my resolution.

Bill predictably grabbed the window seat on the train and turned his head resolutely toward the view that soon whizzed by. I suspect that he was hiding tears, for his hunched shoulders told their own story. How do you convince a nine-year-old that leaving everything behind is a good thing, an adventure? How do I convince myself?

Bill has been lulled to sleep by the swaying of the train, knitting up his raveled sleeve of care after an emotional morning of farewells. Walter mustered the decency to show up at Penn Station and say goodbye to his son in person. However, his resentment at our leaving was painfully obvious and made Bill feel that he was somehow to blame. Perhaps our absence will make Walter's heart grow fonder and he will rally sufficient forgiveness at our desertion for occasional contact if not actual visits—for Bill's sake, if not for his own.

It's a comfort that we are not flying into the unknown but returning to Williams Hill and Grandma's Xanadu. I hope the verdant valley and its "twice five miles of fertile ground" will be an oasis of peace from frenetic

New York, as it has been every summer. And yet, living with nature for summer vacation is one thing, but permanently? What makes me think that I can leave the intellectual stimulation of the city and be content as a country doctor? What makes me think I can save us from the coming climate disaster simply by moving a few hundred miles?

Abby stopped writing, suddenly overwhelmed by doubt that she had made the right decision. Fortunately, her mounting despair was interrupted by the voice of the conductor calling "Providence next, Providence."

She closed the journal and rose from her seat, stretching cramped muscles and running fingers through her short black hair. After tucking book and pen into her backpack, she put a gentle hand on her sleeping son's shoulder. "Put your stuff away; we're almost in Providence."

Bill shrugged away from his mother's hand as if afraid that she would stroke his hair. "Why're we getting off here?" he grumbled, rubbing the sleep out of his eyes. "Why not in Boston, the way we did last time?"

"We talked about this." Then she softened her tone, determined to be patient with her son's anxiety. "We're changing trains here. The new service north toward Worcester is much quicker than going through Boston, and we can get off right in Uxbridge. You'll see; it'll be much more convenient."

"I liked it better when we had a car," he mumbled. The train jerked to a stop, and he spotted a familiar figure standing on the platform. With sudden enthusiasm, he grabbed his pack and was down the aisle before Abby could zip up her own bag.

"Hey, you forgot your coat," she called, but he had already jumped from the steps right into Molly Baker's arms.

"I guess I'm not the only one who's glad to see you," Abby said, joining them. She smiled at the young woman who had been her son's favorite babysitter for several summers and would soon become Abby's colleague.

"I am so honored that you asked me to join your great adventure, Dr. Reed," Molly said, smiling.

"Abby," she reminded her, "unless you want me to call you Nurse Baker."

"Are you really coming to live with us? Not just for the summer?" Bill asked, jumping up and down so hard his freckles threatened to fly right off his nose.

"I'll come up in a couple of weeks, as soon as I graduate. But I couldn't wait to see you and decided to meet your train today."

"You know that we're going to be poor?" Bill warned solemnly.

"I think you got that part wrong," Molly said. "Your Mom is the richest person I have ever met."

Bill examined his mother from top to bottom, contemplating this novel idea. Then he laughed. "Oh, you mean that metaphorically." That was his word for the week, and he used it at every opportunity with surprising aptness.

"Why don't you two sit here and catch up while I wrestle with the baggage and find out where we catch our train home." Abby said.

Home, that sounded so good—so much more comfortable than the fancy West Side brownstone in Manhattan that had never felt quite right.

~»

Abby walked up to the official-looking man who stood next to a large pile of crates and boxes that had obviously just been off-loaded from the departing train. She recognized most of the baggage as hers, mingled with several other crates and trunks.

"How do I get my stuff transferred to the Worcester train?" she asked.

The man removed his shiny new uniform cap with one hand and scratched his head with the other. "We don't do that, lady," he said. "They're not Amtrak, and we don't handle their stuff."

"They assured me in New York that it would be taken care of."

"They didn't tell me nothing 'bout that. This baggage car thing is new. Usually passengers just carry their own luggage with them."

Actually, a baggage car is not new–just the revival of an old idea, Abby thought but did not say aloud.

"May I help you?" a deep voice asked from behind her back.

Abby jumped in surprise and turned around. She squinted up at the handsome man who was silhouetted by the noonday sun. Although she herself was tall, he towered over her. "Why Tom Whittier, is that really you?"

"Yea, it really is me, Dr. Reed–or should I call you Dr. Harrington?"

"I kept my maiden name; Dr. Harrington was my husband." She almost said is. "But you used to call me Abby."

"That was when you were just a squirt of a girl who called me Tommy."

"You've grown much too big for Tommy!"

"Tom will do fine."

The baggage handler interrupted. "If you two lovebirds will stop cooing, what do you intend to do with all this stuff? I can't let you borrow no cart. Besides I ain't got one big enough for all them crates."

Abby quickly explained her difficulty to Tom.

"I have the same problem," he said. "The crates over there are mine. If you're going to Williams Hill, we're on the same train."

He pointed across several tracks. "That's it over there."

"But that's just a freight train," Abby protested.

"Not that one. See the car pulled up at that makeshift wooden platform? It's a retired Amtrak car that they revamped for the new passenger service. They'll couple it to the end of the freight train. I came down on it on Monday, and it's quite comfortable."

Several men approached, bumping two large handcarts along a walkway that crossed several train tracks–the baggage handlers sent to transfer their goods. Tom and Abby pointed out their belongings to the burly men and chatted while they watched them load.

"Have you moved back to Uxbridge?" Abby asked, just as Tom was saying, "Are you going to Williams Hill for the summer?"

"No, my son, Bill, and I are moving there for good. And you?"

"The Williams Hill Council just hired me. They're planning some exciting projects."

"So, you're a building contractor, just like your father?"

"I'm an architect," Tom answered with pride, as if he wanted to impress her.

"I remember the summer you and your father put solar panels on my grandmother's house in Williams Hill. I did hear that you went to Worcester Polytech soon after, but then I lost track."

"My father used to brag about you being at Harvard. After Polytech, I went to MIT School of Architecture and meant to look you up. But I wasn't sure you'd remember me."

"I'd have loved to see you," Abby murmured politely. She looked up at the handsome man before her, amazed that the awkward, lanky teenager had become this self-confident, obviously successful professional. "What did you do after MIT? Didn't I hear something about a prize out west?"

"I spent several years as a resident with the Taliesin West Sustainability Program. The work I did there in exploring putting solar panels on geodesic domes was chosen as a finalist by the Buckminster Fuller Institute in their challenge competition of 2018."

One of the baggage handlers hefted a box and interrupted. "Hey lady, what do you have in here? Rocks?"

Abby blushed. "I'm afraid those are books."

"Why? Who owns books anymore?"

"I do. And be careful of those big crates; they contain sensitive medical equipment."

Tom ignored the interruption. "So, you are moving to Williams Hill. Do you plan to open a practice there?"

She nodded. His friendly smile and questioning look invited a more complete answer, but she didn't want to get into her complicated story just now and was relieved to be interrupted by the approach of Molly and Bill. "This is my old friend, Tom Whittier. He's also taking the train," she said. "Tom, meet Molly Baker. She will be my nursing assistant."

Oh-ho, she thought, when she saw the looks of mutual admiration that sparked between the two.

Abigail was about to introduce her son when Tom squatted down to Bill's eye level. "Hi there. I would have recognized you anywhere–you look just like your mother."

Though Bill was normally shy when meeting strangers, he responded to the friendly greeting and shook hands with a polite, "How-de-do, Mr. Whittier. I'm Bill Harrington. Most people say I look like my father–I get my blue eyes from him."

Abby noticed that he stressed his surname, as if to assert his ties with his father and independence from his mother's shadow.

"Well, Mr. Harrington. If I may call you Bill, my friends know me as Tom. I haven't met your father, but you have your mother's delightful smile."

Bill seemed to grow taller as his small hand was clasped in that of his new friend. Abby remembered that even as a shy teenager, Tom had had the ability to reach out to everyone.

Molly reached up to hug her goodbye and whispered, "He likes you."

"Nah, he's just being friendly," Abby whispered back. But a good beginning, she thought as she took Bill's hand and followed the baggage carts to their train.

~»

There were only a few seats left in the single passenger car, but Tom managed to snare four with a narrow table between them. Bill scooted into one by the window so he could wave goodbye to Molly. Tom stowed their bags overhead and sat down, barely in time to avoid being thrown by the series of jerks as their car was coupled to the end of the freight train. And then they were off.

Abby looked around at the Spartan but serviceable car. Amtrak had retired it as too shabby even for their regional Boston–NY route, but the operators of the brand-new Providence–Worcester passenger route had renovated it with fresh paint and refurbished seats.

In 2018, after a cascade of climate change disasters had devastated New England, the states had despaired of effective federal action to control greenhouse gases and passed their own carbon tax laws. The combination of the steep yearly rise in fees and cost of gasoline had gradually slowed automobile and truck traffic to a trickle of electric cars moving along eerily empty highways. However, the new laws specified that a significant portion of the revenue raised by taxes be used to upgrade rail systems and subsidize their energy costs, thus preventing transportation from coming to a complete standstill.

The Providence–Worcester Rail Company had seized the bonanza of funding to improve service in southern Massachusetts and Rhode Island. It now hauled most of the freight around the region and was replacing the large fleets of trucks that had heretofore clogged the highways. Coupling a passenger car to a freight train on the Providence–Worcester route was a recent innovation, and service had just opened earlier in June.

~»

Bill was still grumpy. "I don't see why we have to take this crummy old train when we could go to Boston first, like we did for spring vacation–or just drive, the way we used to."

Abby didn't want to go into the recent changes in New England economics, so she focused on their lack of a car. "You know Dad got the car–he needs it for his job."

"Why couldn't we just buy a new one? One of those neat electric ones that look like a tadpole? They're awes."

"You mean an electric Elio?" Abby sighed. "We don't need a car in Williams Hill."

"Oh, I forgot. We're going to be poor now. I don't want to be poor."

Abby sighed again. "We talked about this. We aren't going to be poor, we just won't need to spend money, and we certainly don't need a car."

She looked despairingly at Tom. "He just doesn't get it."

"He will, just give him time to settle in."

Tom pulled out a notebook and pencil. "Here, Bill, let me show you why it's better to take this 'crummy old train' than go via Boston." He drew a squiggly line diagonally from the lower left to the upper right corner of the page. Pointing to the lower corner he said, "This is Providence where we are, and here at the other end is Boston." Then he drew another line going left. "And west of Boston is Worcester, and below that Uxbridge and Williams Hill. If we took the train to Boston, it would take almost an hour. Then we'd have to take the commuter rail west to Worcester—another hour—and get from there to Uxbridge. Instead we are going straight north by train." He drew another line up from Providence, completing a triangle. "And, voilà, this way we'll be in Uxbridge in thirty minutes where there will be a ride waiting to take us and our baggage to Williams Hill."

Bill frowned as he studied the diagram. Then he brightened. "I grasp." He hesitated a moment, then added, triumphantly, "But if we went to Boston, we could take the train to Concord and visit Uncle Will and my cousin."

Abby threw her hands up. "I give up. But thanks for trying to divert him. Change really upsets him."

To distract Bill, she said, "Didn't you say that you have a new puzzle with you? Play with that to pass the time."

"I used to have an app on my iPad, but I'm not allowed one anymore," Bill explained to Tom as he drew out a box of puzzle pieces. "This is so retro."

Soon Bill was bent over the table, absorbed in fitting pieces together. Sometimes Abby wished that Bill didn't look so much like his father–the same blond hair falling into his eyes, the same hands. For the hundredth time, she worried that she was making a mistake. Even a sometime-father was better than an absent one. Except that then Bill would have continued to compete with corporate medicine for his mother's attention as well as that of his father. Nervously she fingered her left hand, fiddling with the ring that was no longer there.

"A penny for your thoughts," Tom interrupted. "Tell me about the former Dr. Harrington."

Can he read my mind? "I'd rather hear about your plans for expanding Williams Hill," Abby countered.

"Not only expand the CSA to include all the farms in the valley but reorganize to become self-sufficient and sustainable."

Bill had been eavesdropping and asked, "What's a CSA?"

"The acronym stands for 'Community Sponsored Agriculture,'" Tom explained. "They started out as small community farms that delivered produce to members and sold surplus at farmers' markets."

"You remember, we got food from the Williams Hill CSA last summer," Abby added.

"Right, but I always forget what the letters stand for. I didn't like the kale." Bill's head bent over his puzzle again.

"And Williams Hill needs an architect to tell them how to farm?" *What's with this sarcasm? That's no way to gain friends and influence people.*

Tom laughed. "Absolutely. My major at MIT was city planning with a specialty in sustainability and NetZero buildings. Then at Taliesin West, I applied those principles to smaller towns, especially those closely associated with community farming organizations like the Williams Hill CSA."

"Here let me show you." He pulled out a map and spread it out so it covered both their laps. "The first goal is to become energy independent–update the old solar panels and put new ones on every house and barn that doesn't already have them."

He pointed to a ridge along the eastern slope of the hill that gave its name to the village of Williams Hill. "The old Hall up here is too small and too drafty in the winter; instead we'll build a new and larger Commons that can be the center of community life."

"Like a meetinghouse of old?"

"Exactly–we'll go back to our New England roots and become community centered."

"I hope you won't touch the amphitheater."

"Of course not. The Commons will be at the other end of the ridge, where the Hall is now."

Despite her gloomy mood, Abby was caught in the net of Tom's enthusiasm as he continued pointing and explaining. How typical, she thought. To get a man's attention, ask about his work. But she did admire his passion.

"You said you had arranged for a ride from the station," Abby said. "I thought we had to walk."

Tom hesitated before answering. "I should have asked you first, but I thought Bill would like a treat. The CSA just bought an electric utility vehicle for errands to and from Uxbridge. It's small, so transporting our baggage will probably take two trips. But it's a two-seater so I thought Bill could ride with the driver—the two of us must walk."

"Hey, Bill. Did you hear that? Tom says you can ride in the electric cart from the station."

Bill was so concentrated on his game that Abby had to repeat the news, but then he brightened. "For true? That's awes."

When Tom looked puzzled, Abby explained, " 'Awes' is the latest kid-speak for 'awesome'—sometimes it's hard to keep up."

Tom chuckled. "I know what you mean. The latest in Chicago is 'It's a rock,' used to refer to an obstacle or a chore. I keep thinking the kids are talking about music."

It took Abby a second to figure out the reference.

She leaned back and closed her eyes as a hint that she didn't want to talk anymore. Slowly she drifted off, soothed by the clanking of the wheels on the rails. *Going home, going home,* they seemed to say. *Xanadu, home to Xanadu,* she repeated as if it were a magical incantation.

*

Chapter 2: The Williams Hill CSA

Sunday, June 19, 2022

John Warner barely said hello before reminding me that we were expected at the weekly meeting of the CSA. Because of the heat, we met outside in the amphitheater. Only Bill and I seemed bothered by the mosquitoes; everyone else was immune from working in the fields. Oh, for the days of DEET, or at least a couple of citronella candles!

The place has grown, even since last summer. Although I knew a lot of people, there were still enough new faces and names that I felt quite overwhelmed. And next week a dozen Native American teenagers arrive for their summer internships!

Bill seemed quite at home sitting between Tom and me, but as soon as allowed he scampered off with Ned, his stalwart chum from last summer and (surprise) Tom's daughter, Rebecca. In just the few days we have been here, they have become an inseparable triumvirate.

Becca, everyone calls her. She's six months younger than Bill but already as tall as the two boys. I haven't met or even seen her mother—perhaps she hasn't yet arrived—I wonder if she is Native American. I had not realized that Tom wasn't "hired" for a building project but that he intends to formally join the community as soon as his three-month probation is complete. His election is certain. Not only do we need Tom's skills, but he grew up in Uxbridge and was often here with his father on construction projects, so he's a known quantity—at least to us old-timers. Molly won't have any trouble either—after all, she is a former intern. Of course, Bill and I don't have to wait. Even though we've been "nonresidents," we have always been treated as full members of the CSA—grandmothered-in, you might say.

At a sign from his grandfather, nine-year-old Ned Warner ran down the steps of the amphitheater to ring the chimes and thus signal the gathering silence that began every meeting. John Warner, a member of the Society of Friends, had started the custom when he became director of the Williams Hill CSA. Abby squirmed on the hard stone bench, as restless as her son. Yet, old habits quickly asserted themselves, and she began to listen to the silence and enjoy the spectacular view.

The amphitheater was built into the hillside and patterned after the classical Greek theaters on the Acropolis. Although on a much smaller scale than its progenitors, it easily seated the three hundred residents of Williams Hill and associated farms, with plenty of room to spare for the many visitors who flocked to the summer events. Abby herself had fond memories of attending the plays, poetry readings, and dance performances that were traditionally held in the amphy, as it was affectionately called. She had less fond memories of sitting on its backless stone bleachers and had the foresight to bring cushions for Bill and herself—as had most everyone else.

The amphy was shaded from the setting sun by the woods on the hill at its back. Below them, the sunlight reflected in the windows and off the solar-paneled rooftops of houses in the village. Farther east, the valley fields and scattered farmhouses were bathed in the soft evening glow of midsummer. On a hill beyond the valley, the blades of a cluster of wind turbines circled lazily in the light breeze. Except for the turbines, the view was very much like it had been throughout Abby's childhood when she came to Williams Hill to spend the summer with Grandma Abigail. Overcome with nostalgia, she blinked away her tears. Oh, how she wished Grandma were still here to advise her. Would she have approved of her leaving NY? Would she have understood why it was necessary for her, but mostly for Bill?

Or would she have agreed with Walter that she had abandoned science in favor of peace?

Abby wrenched her attention back to the present and looked down at the foot of the hill. The grid of empty streets inside the Ring, the road that encircled the village, bore mute witness to the fact that everyone came to Saturday meeting—or almost everyone. The lone bicyclist, hastening up the hill toward the amphy, reminded Abby that she needed to dig their bicycles out of the basement. Bill would like to be allowed to freely roam the village, and she needed hers to get to the Tri-River Health Center, which was about a mile away.

Abby's eyes drifted back to contemplate the front row below her and John Warner's broad shoulders. She had had a teenage crush on him ever since he first came to Williams Hill. After graduating from the University of Vermont with a major in agriculture, he had first been an intern at the Intervale Farm Center in Burlington, then a staff member. On a tour of their Indian farm, Grandma Abigail had been impressed by the young man and had brought John to Williams Hill to manage the Nipmuck Demonstration Farm for her new Green Valley Foundation that she had founded for the benefit of the area's Native Americans.

Every summer after that, Abby became John's shadow. When her older brother, Will, teased her about being infatuated with the handsome John, she had dismissed the notion. "He's so scientific," she had explained, "just like Grandpa Tony."

"But Grandpa is a doctor," Will had protested.

"And John is a doctor to the land," she had replied pompously. "He nurtures the health of the fields as if they were his patients. His plantings of the Indian 'Three Sisters' are way cool, and the herbal gardens are awesome. Very scientific."

Will had made a rude noise.

Abby was brought back to the present by a second ringing of the chimes that signaled the start of business. *Why can't I ever focus,* she chided herself. *My thoughts are as undisciplined as a room full of cats.*

John rose from his front-row seat, descended to the stage, and faced the assembly. Still handsome, he had aged well and looked every inch the leader. When Grandma Abigail retired in 2010, he had become director of the Green Valley Foundation that had expanded to include the farms of the Williams Hill Community Supported Agriculture, CSA for short. The demonstration farm began to experiment with sustainable organic farming, using crop rotation to replenish the soil without chemical fertilizers, while the foundation continued to sponsor the summer internship program for disadvantaged Indian teenagers. Soon other farms in the Green Valley joined, and Williams Hill became one large cooperative community, managed by an elected council. John was its chair and had just started his second four-year term. Wouldn't Grandma have been surprised and thrilled that her vision of a peaceful Xanadu evolved into this model for meeting the challenge of climate change by reinventing the idea of a collective community.

John gestured for Abby and Bill to join him on the stage. "Before we make various announcements, I want you all to welcome our own Doc Reed and her son, Bill Harrington."

After the applause had died down, he added, "Of course, you all know Abby as our favorite summer visitor and granddaughter of our fabulous CSA founder, Abigail Palacio, but you may not have heard that she and Bill are to become permanent residents."

John raised his hand to still the buzz of surprise and questions. Abby waved to everyone and spoke briefly, "We are so pleased to become a true part of this great community," she said. "The details of my role in the CSA are still being worked out, but next week, I start at the Tri-River Health Center as a family practitioner. Then as soon as I'm settled there I will start a health maintenance clinic right here in the village, just for members of the CSA."

More applause. Abby and Bill could hardly make their way back to their seats for the well-wishers that surrounded them. Bill was his usual shy self until Ned and Becca started to drag him off.

"Not so fast, young man," Ned's mother said. "I'm about to announce next week's work assignments. All three of you have to stay for those; then you may be excused."

"Aw, Mom, can't you just tell us later?" Ned asked, smiling irresistibly up at his mother.

Apparently, Dee Warner was immune to his charm for she put a restraining hand on her son's shoulder. "You know I won't treat you any differently from the rest; you have to listen with everyone else. Now go and ring the chimes again to call the meeting back to order."

"I don't have to work, do I?" Bill asked Abby nervously. "I never did before."

Becca answered before Abby had a chance, "Around here, everybody has to work. It's a big rock, but even us newcomers aren't free."

"Well, I didn't last year," Bill grumbled.

"Last year we weren't members of the CSA, just summer visitors," Abby pointed out. "But you did work; you just thought it was for fun. Even Dad did, when he was here."

Bill brightened at the mention of his father. "Oh, yeah. He got all sunburned from not wearing his hat." He lowered his voice to a hopeful whisper, "Do you think he's coming this year?"

"I doubt it. He'll be all busy moving to New Jersey and getting settled in his new job."

"Why didn't we go with him? Why'd you say you didn't wanna swim to work?"

"That was a joke, and you weren't supposed to hear it. Little pitchers have big ears."

Bill drew himself up to his full five foot three inches. "I'm not little, and I don't have big ears."

"I know, you are a big boy. Now sit down and put those ears to use. We'll talk about it later."

The acoustics were superb, and Dee had no trouble being heard by everyone. She was the "banker" for the Time Bank and in charge of distributing work assignments for the CSA. Abby didn't envy Dee the task of juggling the needs of the community with everyone's capabilities and requests for plum assignments—talk about herding cats. Although some members had fixed indoor jobs, during the growing season everyone was expected to work some shifts in the fields. Even Abby, despite her job at Tri-River Health Center, was not exempt. She would tend the herbs gardens, much as she had every summer. Medicinal herbs were her passion to which she devoted much of her spare as well as work time.

Bill, like the other preteens, belonged to a quint, supervised by an older teen. During summer vacation, they were assigned to work in the fields but, being children, they were limited to short shifts and had plenty of time to play and otherwise get into trouble.

Abby was glad to see that her son was in a quint with Ned and Becca—that would please him. She was not so sure that Max, their current teen leader, would be as pleased; Ned tended to be rambunctious, and Bill often interpreted authority per his own lights.

Abby tried hard to pay attention, but she was soon lost in the jumble of names of team leaders and work group supervisors, and her mind wandered to planning the expansion of the medicinal herb garden. The increasingly stringent funding of Medicare and rising cost of insurance was having an impact on the price and availability of drugs, and she was convinced that they would soon be priced out of the reach of most people. Her erstwhile hobby of herbals might soon have to be put to practical use with her own patients, and a serious study of traditional medicines could make an essential contribution to the health of the community.

Now, where in Grandma's library would I find Healer Bess's seventeenth-century journal? She wrote something about sassafras root for—

A pounding on her knee abruptly interrupted her daydream. "So, can we go now?" Bill was saying.

Abby had barely grunted her assent before the three musketeers ran off. "Be back at sunset," she called after them.

"And don't go into the woods," Tom added, a nervous edge to his voice. With the children gone, he had shifted over so he was sitting next to Abby.

Abby turned to reassure him. "They'll be fine; Ned knows they're not allowed in the woods alone, and Bill has an incredible internal navigation system."

"Yes, but it'll be dark soon—and Becca easily panics."

"You worry about her too much. This is a safe place—no street violence like in the cities."

"Perhaps you're right. I do worry about her. The gangs are bad in Chicago, and likely to get worse with the heat of summer. The escalating violence is one of the reasons I wanted to bring Becca back here."

"New York's even worse. Especially after the food riots—the hot summers don't help. But you know what they say about it taking a village to raise a child. You couldn't ask for a better one than Williams Hill."

Apparently, Dee had finished talking, for she sat down and John took the floor again. "I am glad to announce that the state has finally agreed to let us take over the management of the Nipmuck Forest and integrate it into our research in sustainable agriculture. That means we can gather nuts and berries and let our animals forage for acorns in the fall, using the Indian principles of conservation."

"What's that?" Abby whispered.

"The Indians had a tradition of not stripping every bush, but always left something behind for the birds and other wildlife," Tom replied.

John let the applause die down and gestured for Steve Browne to rise. "Steve has agreed to be our forest manager and tree-hugger-in-chief. Speak to him if you want to join his team or have any questions. But remember, the forest belongs to everyone, not just members of the CSA—we agreed to conduct tours for the public."

"Before we adjourn, I have a few more announcements," John continued. "First some really good news. According to the Global

Carbon Project, not only are CO2 emissions down worldwide, but the percentage from renewable sources has risen to twenty-five percent in the U.S.—on track to meet our national goal of at least fifty percent by 2035."

He held up his hand to forestall the applause that threatened to erupt. "Furthermore, NOAA reports that although last year the concentration of atmospheric CO2 reached a record 410 parts per million, that is a trivial increase from the year before. Even in the US, energy use is down, though we lag behind the rest of the developed world in reducing greenhouse gas emissions, thanks to continuing obstructionist Washington politics. However, we can take pride in the fact that New England continues to lead the effort, and Williams Hill has shown the way it can be done."

Now the cheers were unrestrained. When they finally died, John reminded everyone that during the continuing heat wave, no one was allowed to work outside at midday. "Siestas are strongly recommended, especially for children and the elderly. The alarm bell will sound whenever the temperature exceeds a hundred, and as soon as the Hall has been air-conditioned, it'll be open, even during construction, for anyone seeking to cool off."

Dee raised her hand.

"Oh, yes, last but not least," John said. "Next weekend is our ever-popular Midsummer Festival. Because of the new passenger train, we can expect a bigger attendance than the last couple of years, including several members of Food Solutions New England. They will be here for a week as guests of the foundation. This is our chance, once again, to show off our village on the hill and what we are trying to accomplish. Also, the twelve Pokanoket teenagers will arrive from Bristol, Rhode Island, for their summer internships; all but two have been here before. Some are bringing their parents for the weekend. If you're signed up to host, please speak to Dee for the names of your guests. Sarah tells me that there is a meeting of the festival committee on Monday night. If you haven't yet volunteered, just show up. In the Hall if it rains, otherwise right here?" He looked questioningly at his wife in the front row. "I see that's a yes."

"Are there any other announcements?" John scanned the gathering. "Well then, we are done. Who's leading tonight's storytelling?"

Tom turned to Abby. "Are you staying?"

"No, I'm too tired," she said. "I'm not used to getting up at dawn."

"That's what siestas are for." Tom said. "If you're going back to Hexagon House, I'll walk with you, if I may."

"So, you think I need an escort? I told you that it's safe here." *Do I have to be so rude?*

"No, I don't think you need anyone. I'd just like to walk with you."

Is he hitting on me? Striving for a more pleasant voice, Abby repeated that she was too tired.

Tom was not to be put off. "We don't have to talk; we can just walk." He offered his hand, ostensibly to help her navigate down the steps to the path down to the village center. "It's such a beautiful evening."

"It is that," Abby said, taking his hand.

*

Chapter 3: Doc Reed and Nurse Molly

Sunday, July 17, 2022

What a week! Though my office at the Tri-River Health Center is reasonably well set up, I am still trying to figure out the politics. I thought I was escaping the jungle of Industrial Health, but the center, though on an infinitely smaller scale, has its own politics of personalities and procedures to navigate. Some of my new colleagues appear to resent me, as if they fear that I'm a snobbish "Harvard" doctor–or maybe they think I'll steal their patients. Considering the jam in the waiting room, I don't think that's a problem. I do have some allies, rallied on my behalf by Betty, who reminded them that I have been helpful during crises in the past. She has been invaluable in steering me through the hazards of the record-keeping system for the New England universal health insurance plan that everyone calls NewECare. I'm too used to handing reimbursements over to support staff, but navigating around the shoals of new forms is too much for our lone Rob, so doctors and nurses must fill out most of their own. A former trucking company manager, Rob was laid off when it closed and is almost as much of a novice as I to NewECare.

Molly arrived last Saturday and will be living with us, at least for the time being. Bill is, of course, thrilled to have her here, though I should remind him that she is not his babysitter anymore–more like an older sister and part of the family.

On Monday, Molly started work at the center and is a treasure–the shyest patient warms to her immediately, and she has a way of engaging children's attention so they don't notice needles. When I asked her where she had learned to handle patients that way, she gave me the credit! She hardly needs any supervision, and it's difficult to know who is learning more, student or mentor. Her training at accelerated nurse practitioner program in Providence was superb, and I'm grateful to have her on my side. She insisted on everyone addressing me as "Dr. Reed," though I would have been happy with "Abby." "Here at the center we must maintain a professional distance if the patients are to trust us with their lives," she said firmly. You'd think she had gray hair and was at least ten years my senior! "The whole point of coming here was for me to be closer to my patients," I protested. We finally compromised on "Doc Reed."

Abby had first met Molly in Bristol four years earlier, when Hurricane Ralph devastated the Connecticut and Rhode Island coasts. Abby had volunteered at the Pokanoket Indian Clinic during several previous summers and knew that low-lying Bristol, on a spit of land in Narragansett Bay, was particularly vulnerable. On hearing the prediction of a major disaster, she had organized a New York medical rescue team. No sooner had they arrived in Bristol after a harrowing twelve-hour trip in a commandeered minibus, before she was called to a medic tent to examine a Native American woman whose leg had been crushed.

A quick look told Abby that the leg was beyond rescue; although a tourniquet had been applied, the lower end of the stretcher was soaked in blood. All she could do was stabilize her patient enough for transport to the nearest hospital. She asked the woman her name.

"Mother can't hear you," said a teenage girl who squatted on the other side of the stretcher clutching the woman's hand. "They gave her a shot for the pain."

"You'd be surprised what she might be able to hear."

"Dawn. Her name is Dawn Baker," the girl said. "I'm Molly," she added politely. Her voice sounded composed although her face was white. Her eyes were red from weeping and her pupils dilated. The girl was probably in shock.

"Please make sure Molly is all right," Abby whispered to the nurse at her side.

"I'm fine," Molly protested and refused to budge. "I have to stay right here."

Abby bent over the woman. "Dawn, I'm Dr. Reed. I'm going to help you."

She readjusted the tourniquet and carefully removed the fragments of bone and tissue that had obscured the source of the bleeding. While gesturing for a suture kit so she could tie off the damaged artery, she said, "Molly, tell me about you and your mother while I work." That would help take the girl's mind off the immediate danger.

Apparently, Molly was going to be a senior at Bristol High School next month and had three younger siblings. The father was a fisherman, part owner of a trawler. He and his crew had sailed out to sea to ride out the storm–they were still missing. The Baker family's small shack had been flattened by a tree and then nearly swept away by the storm surge that came roaring up the Bay.

"What about your siblings? Are they safe?"

"Mom had taken us to the shelter at school. She went back to find our cat—" Molly was unable to go on. Suddenly she jumped up, her voice panicky, "When they told me about Mom, I just left the kids there–I have to go back."

"I'm sure they're fine–they'll take good care of them at the shelter. But if you like, we can send someone to check–or you can go."

"No, no. I have to stay," Molly repeated, contradicting herself and sitting down again.

She gathered herself remarkably quickly. She watched Abby's hands, absorbing her every move. "What you're doing is amazing. Your hands are so sure; your stitching is as fine as my mother's sewing."

"Your mother sews?" Anything to distract the girl. "Do you?"

As if she hadn't heard, Molly said, "I'd love to do that–be a doctor."

"Why not? Are you a good student?"

"Yes, but there's no money for college even. I want to graduate high school, but after that, Mom tells me, I'll need to get a job." She looked down at her mother's shattered leg and the reality of a grim future silenced her.

"I've done what I can," Abby said, removing the tourniquet and turning to the EMT hovering in the background.

"If she's ready, we're transporting her to Miriam Hospital in Providence," he said.

"St. Anne's in Fall River is closer–Mrs. Baker is barely stable," Abby objected.

The EMT pushed the gurney toward the back of the ambulance. "The bridge to Fall River is out," he called over his shoulder. "The storm surge destroyed all but a few pilings. We'll be lucky to make it to Providence."

"Good luck. We just came down from there and the road is pretty bad."

Seeing Molly start to get into the ambulance, the EMT said firmly, "No kid, you can't come. There's no room. We need to fit two more gurneys in there."

"I have to be with her," Molly protested. "I have to make sure she's alright."

Abby put a restraining arm around the girl's shoulders. "Let them do their job. Yours is to stay here with your siblings and wait for your father to come home."

"I don't think he made it. What'll we do if he doesn't?" she wailed, leaning into Abby.

What indeed?

Abby comforted the girl as best she could. Eventually, she found a Red Cross volunteer and asked her to bring Molly back to the shelter. She returned to the tent to concentrate on her next patient, a little boy with a broken arm.

~»

Even after Abby went back home to New York, she kept in touch with Molly. Such a sad story with such a happy ending. The ambulance taking Mrs. Baker to Providence was first stuck in the traffic of people fleeing north, then had to take a long detour because the highway was flooded. Dawn had lost too much blood to survive and died soon after arriving at the hospital. However, Molly's father and crew were safe. They were towed into Falmouth Harbor by the Coast Guard after being adrift for two days. The crew was hungry although otherwise fine, but the boat was badly damaged. Fred Baker left it in the boat yard and rushed home to find his family in shambles.

Meanwhile, Molly and her siblings had lived at the shelter, anxiously waiting for their father's return. Concerned for them, Abby talked to Molly over the phone and then with her father. In consultation with John Warner back in Williams Hill, she arranged for the temporary fostering of the children with families in Williams Hill until Mr. Baker could get his life back together. Molly went with them and stayed with the Warners to see them settled. That fall, Bristol schools started late, but Molly was determined to fulfill her mother's wish for her by graduating, and in late September she went home to her father's FEMA trailer. The children were well cared for in Williams Hill, so Fred Baker reluctantly decided to let them stay there until he could find more suitable housing.

It took a year, but with the help of the Pokanoket Tribe's lawyers, Fred Baker maneuvered through the red tape of collecting the insurance on both his house and boat. By next June, Molly had graduated with high honors from Bristol High School, and the boat repairs were finished. While Fred went back to fishing, Molly came to Williams Hill as a summer intern.

In the fall, Fred found a house with enough room for the family to be reunited and the children returned to Bristol. With Abby's strong recommendation and a scholarship from the Green Valley Foundation, Molly was admitted to the new accelerated nursing program at Rhode Island College in Providence. The program was especially designed to help the nursing crisis by providing education for talented minority students. The curriculum consisted of three full years of class work, followed by a rigorously supervised internship with an approved practicing physician. Abby Reed was, of course, more than qualified and readily agreed to be Molly's mentor.

The evening of Molly's arrival at Williams Hill, Abby introduced her to the CSA members at the regular Saturday meeting. "Please welcome our own Molly Baker," she said. "She has just finished all but the practicum for her nursing degree and will be my assistant here in Williams Hill and at the Tri-River Health Center. She wants to say a few words."

Molly smiled at the friendly crowd. "I cannot tell you how welcome you have all made me feel already, and I want to thank you and the foundation from the bottom of my heart for sponsoring my studies and for giving me the opportunity to be a part of this amazing community. I am especially grateful to Dr. Reed for being my mentor and for giving me a place to live."

~»

Hurricane Ralph changed both Molly and Abby's lives profoundly but had a much wider effect in triggering what became known as the "Carbon Rebellion." In 2018, when Ralph came roaring up the Atlantic coastline, it devastated southern Connecticut but destroyed Narragansett Bay and bankrupted Rhode Island. Environmental activists of the Save-the-Bay organization put the blame squarely on climate change and rallied the large numbers of displaced people living in FEMA camps. They stormed the statehouse in Providence chanting "Never again" and insisting that the stalled state carbon tax be passed. The legislature bowed under the pressure and, in emergency session, finally acted.

The following October, mega-storm Clarence dumped torrential rains on central New England, flooding the rivers, including the Mystic and the Charles. When the power grid failed, so did the pumps on the dams between the Charles and Boston Harbor. The streets of Boston's Back Bay were awash, and Beacon Hill nearly an island. The next day, a massive flotilla of canoes converged on the submerged Esplanade at the foot of Beacon Hill, waving green flags, chanting "Save Boston" and singing Guthrie's "This Land Is Your Land," nicknamed the "Green Battle Hymn." Though order was restored relatively quickly, by November the receding waters carried Patrick O'Brien and his environmental platform into office as governor of Massachusetts. By spring, the Bay State and Connecticut fell to the "Carbon Rebellion" that soon united all of New England. Imports, extraction, and transport of fossil fuels in the region were heavily taxed.

The fossil fuel industry cried "foul" and protested "restraint of trade." Fortunately, the extraction industry was unable to get a restraining order, and the carbon tax remained in place while the lawsuits wove their ponderous way through the layers of state and federal courts. Meanwhile, the environmental lobby in Washington succeeded in halting federal oil subsidies and rolled those moneys over to stimulate the clean energy industry.

In 2019, Maine, reacting to the continuing dismantling of the federal Affordable Care Act, passed single-payer health legislation similar to the one already in place in Vermont. When Republican President Jackson took office the following year, the other four New England states followed suit, and the New England Comprehensive Health Care Act was born, becoming known as NewECare.

BRIAN BURT

United States

Brian Burt writes both short- and novel-length fiction. He has published more than twenty science fiction and fantasy stories in various magazines and anthologies. His short story "The Last Indian War" won the Writers of the Future Gold Award and was included in *Writers of the Future Volume VIII*. His debut novel, *Aquarius Rising Book 1: In the Tears of God*, won EPIC's 2014 eBook Award for Science Fiction. *Aquarius Rising Book 2: Blood Tide* won the Readers' Favorite Gold Medal for Science Fiction in 2016. Burt works as a cybersecurity engineer and lives with his wife, three sons, a mongrel puppy, and an adopted stray cat in idyllic Southwest Michigan. The cat, in particular, remains unimpressed with his literary efforts unless they come with tuna.

STORM RIDER

a short story

The storm didn't howl. Not yet. It hissed and spat and growled low in the throat of the swollen sky, occasionally rising to an eerie whistle, like wind blowing through a graveyard. That made sense to Rick Harvey. The entire town of Requiem was a grave now; a desolate ruin haunted by gray, uneasy ghosts. Its former residents had abandoned it, one way or another. The lucky ones moved away after the devastation. The unlucky had been reaped by the whirlwind, some of their bodies never recovered.

And—in more ways than he could count—Rick had never recovered either.

He chased dark memories back into the shadows of his mind, tried to focus on the task at hand. He waded through the rising seawater that regularly drowned this section of the town, inspecting his instrument packages and sensor arrays. The Beachview Drive neighborhood had deteriorated since the last big storm. Many of the older, traditional houses collapsed into moldering, algae-covered piles of rubble, their foundations covered in barnacles. Rick's former house—his meticulously engineered, state-of-the-art, stormproof refuge against the wrath of Mother Nature—still stood. But not unscathed. He sloshed toward it, bent against the wind: an elevated, eggshell-colored geodesic dome looking like a structure out of science fiction, something from a lunar colony. He clomped up the entrance steps and turned the handle on the front door. A sudden, violent gust nearly blew the door off its hinges as it banged open, the handle sliding out of his rain-soaked hand. He slipped inside, managed to shoulder the door shut and bolt it against the storm. A futile gesture. One of the ocean-facing windows had been completely knocked out of its frame; rain shot through the opening like liquid bullets, lashing the South Florida coast more horizontally than vertically. Rick stared at the single pane of shatterproof acrylic on the floor beneath the naked frame, remembering. Trying desperately not to.

The storm was getting bad. The images that flashed through his brain like lightning, jolting the tender, wounded parts of him, were worse.

Rick wove through the house's drunken interior geometries, picking his way among debris littering the stained floor, verifying that the power packs on the instruments mounted to the curved exterior walls were fully charged. No way to plug into the grid here. FPL had long ago abandoned any attempts to restore power to a ghost town now infamous as "the hurricane magnet of the Gulf Coast." The wags on the Weather Channel would be trotting that one out repeatedly in the next forty-eight hours. Who could blame them? Three direct hits from hurricanes in the past fifteen years, plus two tropical storms. It defied the odds, defied common sense. That alone would have been more than the most weatherworn Floridians could bear. But nobody—nobody foresaw the impact of Diego, the Hand of God. No. The Hand of Satan.

Rick tugged at a sensor, making sure it was firmly attached, and brushed a mist of saltwater out of his brown hound-dog eyes. *This time, he would be ready. This time would be different!*

A distinctive ringtone chimed insistently. Rick fumbled with the sealed pouch inside his slicker and tugged out his smartphone, pressing it tightly to his ear. "Yeah."

"Rick? How's it looking?"

"Not bad. I've checked all of the equipment deployed in the Beachview zone. Half a dozen sensors down due to failed power supplies or faulty electronics, but everything else is online and functional. We should get good data from this one, Mel."

Melanie Rodriguez was a professor of meteorology and physical oceanography at the University of Miami's Rosenstiel School of Marine and Atmospheric Science. She was also one of Rick Harvey's dearest friends, that rare colleague in whom he still confided. One of the few people who hadn't cut him loose in the aftermath of Diego. He heard the worry in her voice, despite the wind and pelting rain.

"Rick, this one's going to be bad. The latest spaghetti plot shows Ileana hitting you dead-center. It's projected to be at least a Cat-Four when it hits, the worst since Diablo— I mean, Diego." There was a long, awkward pause. "I'm sorry, Rick. Slip of the tongue."

Not her fault, of course, Rick reminded himself as the nickname sank its fangs into his chest and injected venom into his heart. Hurricane Diego had forever become Diablo in the minds of Floridians–of the nation, who observed its carnage vicariously through the media–after a Miami weatherman coined the term. It was a moniker worthy of a cyclone so destructive that it had prompted NOAA to create a Category Six on the Saffir-Simpson Hurricane Wind Scale. Only the devil could have spun up a storm so cruel and callous, a storm that had consigned Rick's soul to its own special hell. Mel knew that all too well.

"Rick? You still there?"

"Yeah. Hard to hear, though; cell reception's degrading fast."

"That's why I'm calling, Rick. Look, you don't need to be on-site to monitor the data; the sensors will collect and record everything whether you're next door or half a state away. I vote for half a state away. You've done your job, now head inland and get out of harm's way."

"Something might go wrong here. I need to be close enough to react."

"BS, brother. If something goes south when the eye wall hits, you won't be able to do a damn thing besides batten down the hatches and pray. Come on, Rick; abandon ship. Please."

Rick Harvey sighed—a sad, resigned sound swallowed by the storm. He stared at the phone's luminous screen, tempted to disconnect the call.

"Rick, talk to me. I know you're there!"

"I have to stay, Mel. You know that."

Rick heard a muffled obscenity stifled by a groan. "Dammit, you're not meant to die in that place. That's not what Shannon or Marta would want, and you know it."

"No," he said. "They'd want me to make sure it doesn't happen again to somebody else's family. That's what I'm doing. I plan to head out of town any minute now and ride this out in the Hobbit House, just like we discussed. If my structural improvements pan out in the new model, I'll be safer than you are in Dade."

"And if they don't, you could get blown into the Glades," said Mel. They both fell silent for a long moment, serenaded by the storm. "Ah, hell— I have faith in you, even if you are a bloody fool. Stay safe, Rick. Call me with updates if you can get a signal."

"Sure. And, Mel—you stay safe, too. Miami's gonna feel this one."

"Not like you will over there, my friend." That, thought Rick, was true on many levels. "See you on the other side." She disconnected and Rick's phone screen dimmed to black. Overall, it was a perfect reflection of his mood. He stole one last look around what Marta had lovingly called the Igloo, a space crowded with memories–angels and demons grappling for dominance–before heading for the door.

Back in the lashing rain, wading through floodwaters that swirled over the cracked pavement and around the rusted hulks of abandoned cars, Rick turned from the line of houses that stretched away like rows of rotting teeth and struggled to get his bearings. To the north, he spotted the highest point in Requiem rising, gray and ghostly, toward the clouds. His destination. He slogged through the foaming vanguard of Hurricane Ileana in the direction of what locals had once called Heartache Hill: a massive, lumpy mound bulldozed into existence above the flat plain of the town, a monument to tragedy assembled from the wreckage accumulated from Requiem's obliterated neighborhoods. FEMA contractors had hauled load after load of debris to the place, pushing the pile toward heaven like a shattered offering, a prayer for mercy upon the huddled survivors below. That prayer had fallen on deaf ears. Nobody–not the Feds, the state authorities, not even the most loyal residents–seriously considered rebuilding what had been lost.

No matter. In a way, that made this the perfect laboratory for somebody like Rick Harvey. He trudged doggedly toward the distant hill, relieved to have the winds shoving at his back. He wasn't focused on rebuilding. He wanted to build something new.

He reached the base of the hill, a midden of discarded dreams and buried nightmares. The sandy topsoil of the hill lay etched with shallow lines and crisscross trenches eroded by rivulets of runoff; torrential rains tumbled down the sides, exposing patches of detritus underneath. Rick scrambled upward, slipping and sliding, crawling on all fours. The storm intensified. Time was running out. Halfway up, the Hobbit House peeked from between curtains of rain.

Rick reached the rows of solar panels first, confirmed that they were lowered and stowed in their protective ditch below ground level. Banks of Powerwall batteries beneath the house stored all the juice he'd stockpiled before the storm moved in; backup generators would see him through the duration, if Ileana stalled over the coast and hid the sun for days. The rounded contours of the Hobbit House jutted from the hillside just beyond the solar array. He could have built on the northeastern face of Heartache Hill, on the leeward side protected from the worst battering of stormy fists that pummeled Requiem from the coast. That would have been a cheat, a coward's way out. Rick exposed his newest experimental house to the brunt of any hurricane rolling in from the Gulf. That was the point: to fight the devil face to face.

Still, he wasn't crazy. The house sat far above the reach of any storm surge. The back part of the monolithic dome was recessed into the hillside; a ring of steel posts supported the front part of the dome, extending deep into concrete-filled boreholes. Rick ducked between the posts, clambered up the metal stairs that led to the entrance chamber in the floor. No front door was buffeted directly by gale-force winds; the door above the grate stairs lay hidden in a storage room that doubled as a coat closet. Rick shrugged out of his slicker, hung it on the rack, then closed and sealed the watertight hatch reserved for the deadliest weather. Like taking refuge in a submarine, or maybe a nuclear bunker. Not stylish, not elegant— but Rick Harvey cared more about saving lives than appearing in the Parade of Homes. He was willing to go to any length to prove his theories, with one exception: he refused to risk any lives besides his own.

That was a lesson he had learned the hard way.

He opened the inner door, crossed the modest, utilitarian kitchen, and entered his office at the front of the house. Thick acrylic windows were set into the exterior wall, as well as a circular skylight in the ceiling, perfectly matching the curvature of the dome itself. Clouds roiled and writhed overhead, blurred by the relentless, splattered shrapnel of the rain. As the eye of Ileana drew closer, she blinded human eyes. Rick had better ways to observe the storm. His gaze swiveled to the flatscreen TV where he'd projected satellite images of Ileana's progress. A vortex spun in the center of the screen, a psychedelic spiral galaxy with bands of color indicating different wind speeds. The eye was less than fifty miles offshore. Rick studied the metrics. Not a large system, more Andrew's scale than Floyd's; the diameter of hurricane-force winds extended less than fifty miles. But the winds at the center were intense, sustaining speeds above 175 miles per hour. No monster size-wise—but monstrous in terms of sheer, concentrated destructive power. Ileana had strengthened into a Category-Five juggernaut, an irresistible force capable of flattening everything in her path.

According to the latest plots, that path aimed the lethal core of the cyclone's fury directly at the skeletal remains of Requiem.

A wave of vertigo swept over Rick, left him nauseous and

trembling, paralyzed by a PTSD flashback to ten years ago. He and Marta and his sweet, elfin Shannon huddled on the lumpy couch of the family room in the Igloo, staring at satellite images that danced on their television screen while a meteorologist's shrill, excited voice pronounced their doom. Unusually warm waters in the Gulf pumped massive energies into Diego; instead of the Cat Three forecast by most models, the storm continued to strengthen. They nibbled blue-corn tortilla chips and stale trail mix and watched, rapt and horrified, as the hurricane climbed the ladder: Category Four, Category Five. When sustained winds rose above 230 miles per hour, Diego became something unprecedented. It seemed to Rick, at the time, as if a hurricane had violated a tornado, spawning a misbegotten obscenity unlike anything in the annals of recorded weather history. Diablo was born. Diablo bore down on the homes of Requiem like a laser-guided missile. And it was far too late for anyone to flee—

The wind outside the Hobbit House crescendoed to a howl. Was history poised to repeat itself? Rick shook himself out of his stupor, dismayed but determined. "Bring it, bitch."

This time, he had nothing left to lose.

He grabbed his laptop, booted the custom program he'd developed to aggregate the readings from all of the instrumentation he'd painstakingly installed throughout the marinated ruins of what had once been downtown Requiem. Red lights flashed everywhere on his computer screen, as if the program's dashboard had been shot full of bullet holes with an assault rifle. Mel was right, of course; he'd get no telemetry from the sensors until the storm abated—if, of course, the instruments survived. *And if I survive to upload the data.* Sadly, at that moment, his fading internet connection also gave up the ghost. The satellite image on his TV screen froze and then evaporated as an error message filled the screen in its place.

He was completely cut off. Nothing left to do but hunker down and ride the storm.

Rick retreated to the rear of the Hobbit House, to the sheltered chamber nestled beneath the hillside that doubled as a study and a bedroom. He grabbed a bottle of Black Bush from the liquor shelf and a smudged glass from the low hardwood table in the center of the room, filled it to the brim, drained half of it with one swig that made his eyes water. He plunked the whiskey bottle down on the table to keep it close, flinched when some piece of windblown wreckage collided against the shell of the dome with a thunderous, ringing thud, and gulped another swallow. Bushmills was essential storm gear. It infused him with courage even while conditions worsened, dulled the razor edge of memories that prowled at the back of his mind, eager to shred his self-control. Rick plopped down on the futon sofa, laptop in one hand, nearly empty glass of whiskey in the other. He pulled up the Hobbit House smart-home dashboard, studied readings from the sensors embedded in the walls of the dome; wind pressure rising, frequency of debris collisions rising in lockstep. The ruins of Requiem provided plenty of ammunition to feed Ileana's rage, jagged projectiles she could hurl with deadly force. He drank off the rest of the Black Bush, refilled the glass with hands grown queerly steady. This was the test he'd been waiting for. No regrets. He switched to iTunes and started his very special playlist. The raucous, ragged beat of REO Speedwagon's "Ridin' the Storm Out" blasted from the study's speakers.

Rick chuckled as he drank. Requiem, Florida, was a far cry from the Rockies—but the sentiment still fit. He sat back as Ileana's killer eye wall rolled ever closer–as more debris smashed against the walls of the dome and the wind's howl rose to a relentless, freight-train roar–and listened to the music. The Scorpions screamed at him, shouting down the storm, promising to rock him like a hurricane.

Rick sang along with the repeating, defiant soundtrack and drank, flinching at the perilous percussion of wind-blown missiles launched against the walls of his shelter. Eventually, despite Ileana's banshee wail, he didn't so much doze as pass out after the bottle of Bushmills became the storm's first casualty. His very own liquid first responder, killed in action. *May both of us rest in peace—*

But Rick didn't rest peacefully at all.

He tossed and moaned on the futon, haunted by memories no longer held at bay, nightmares released by booze and guilt and the dissonant symphony of storms. Marta sitting in the middle of that lumpy seashell-patterned couch on Beachview Drive with Shannon cradled in her lap; their little girl terrified, crying softly, wisps of sun-bleached hair matted against her forehead by sweat and tears, clutching a silver dolphin plushy tight against her chest. No escape from that image. His wife whispering words of comfort, trying to be stoic, her tanned arms trembling despite the reassurance in her voice. Rick stalking the room like a caged panther, checking instruments, promising them both above Diablo's screech that everything would be fine. It wouldn't be fine. He was a liar and a fraud. It would be the exact, soul-shattering opposite of fine.

Then the crash—a bomb of debris exploding, shaking the walls in the dream world and the real world simultaneously—and Rick Harvey jerked awake with a scream of terror. Jim Morrison's moody baritone mocked him in the background with the opening verse of "Riders on the Storm."

Rick cradled his head in his hands, sobbing uncontrollably, grief leaking from his eyes like Ileana's storm surge, a force of nature that had to run its course. A decade. A decade since he'd made the biggest mistake of his life. He'd been so certain, so confident that his construction techniques were sound, that his dome-home on Beachview Drive was indestructible. He'd been determined to demonstrate his brilliance to peers, to critics, to everyone. He risked his family to prove the point. The Igloo—the geodesic dome design—was almost perfect. Almost. Except for the windows. He put shatterproof plexiglass in all of them, but he made a fatal design mistake. The windows were fitted in standard frames, not recessed into the walls to provide extra protection against debris strikes. Still, a glancing blow in any normal hurricane would have been deflected harmlessly aside. A glancing blow—Any normal hurricane—Along came Diego, which morphed into Diablo, the avatar of Mother Nature's wrath. A three-foot rod of rebar broke loose from the wreckage of another Beachview property. Diablo hurled that javelin of steel with surgical precision, its point striking one of the Igloo's front windows directly in its center, popping the entire sheet of plexiglass out of its frame. Continuing its path toward the center of the Harveys' seashell couch, while Rick prowled the border of the room ten feet away. Too far to intervene. Too near to forget the sound, the sight, the horrible, irredeemable finality—

Rick's obsession hadn't been born in the Hobbit House. It was born in the Igloo on Beachview Drive; born of tragedy and loss. Jim Morrison and The Doors sang hauntingly of storm riders, of birth and death. Rick was ready to die here to save others.

He curled up on the futon–as empty as the bottle of Black Bush toppled on the wooden table–while Ileana shrieked and clawed at the dome above his bowed head, impotent this time to reach him. Eventually, the freight-train roar faded to a serpent's hiss. Ileana swept inland, most of her fury spent, her power diminished to the gusty winds and drenching rains of a tropical storm. The worst was over. The Hobbit House survived. Rick tugged the laptop onto his lap and pulled up readings from the home's array of monitors. The walls withstood Ileana's onslaught, battered but not breached. The sturdier windows and skylight had survived. Victory. A Pyrrhic victory, of course; Rick lost his war ten years ago.

He switched from the smart-home dashboard to the portal that allowed him to monitor readings from all of the instrument packs deployed around Requiem. Agents reestablished communication with the server; sensors transmitted readings they'd accumulated during the blackout. Rick watched the wealth of data scroll across his screen. Lots of useful metrics here. Mel and her colleagues at the U would be thrilled to see this; they'd pore over the dataset like rabid wolves chasing down a deer. Rick was gratified, but most of the data didn't particularly interest him at the moment. He only cared about one set of readings from one very specific structure. With a few key presses and mouse clicks, he navigated to the data stream from a Beachview Drive address forever burned into his brain.

His fingers tripped and trembled as he scrolled through different files, hunting for the audio recordings. Why? Because of what he'd uncovered, painstakingly and with steadily eroding skepticism, during the past three storm events. No one would believe him. Hell, he barely believed it himself. But, if a picture was worth a thousand words, then an audio recording was worth at least five hundred. He pulled up the first audio file, captured in the deserted family room of the Igloo. He studied the time line on the recording; based on past experience, he fast-forwarded to the midpoint, to the height of Ileana's rage. He tweaked the controls to suppress certain bands in the audio spectrum, to heighten and isolate others. His hands, his arms, his whole body shook. *Grow a spine, Rick!* With a long, shuddering exhalation, he managed to press Play. The sardonic Storm-Rider playlist lapsed into silence, replaced by a series of muted, whispered entreaties in voices that he recognized at once; voices that cut Rick Harvey to the bone.

"Help, Rick."

"Help, Daddy."

He'd expected it—and, still, the phantom susurrations froze the breath in his lungs, stilled the beating of his heart. *Marta. Shannon.* He knew those voices from his sweetest dreams, his most damning nightmares. He would share the rest of the data with other researchers. Not this. This was Rick's private treasure, his precious penance, his alone to suffer and to savor. He rose, unsteadily, wishing that he hadn't drained the bottle of Bushmills. He stumbled across the room to the bookshelves; to one specific shelf, a makeshift shrine erected in the center. Tears blurred his vision as he fought to focus on two mementos on that altar to the past. A tarnished bronze statue of the Wiccan triple goddess: *Marta*. A tattered, goggle-eyed octopus plush toy: *Shannon*. For a moment—one rare, elusive, agonizing moment—they were reunited.

Then his phone rang, insistent and invasive, to shatter the fragile spell. When Rick dragged the phone out of his pocket, Mel's photo filled the screen. He shuddered, sighed, pressed the button to accept the call.

"Hey, Mel."

"Hey? Jesus, Rick, I've been worried sick over here. We were all watching this thing swell into a monster, saw it headed straight for you, and we couldn't get through to warn you. I was freaking out here, you inconsiderate bastard! Why didn't you call me?"

Rick shrugged, vaguely aware that the gesture did no good on a choppy audio call. Not really caring. "I just got cell service back. I've been uploading the data feeds, analyzing metrics from the sensors. We've got some great stuff this time around. And, yes:

the Hobbit House performed as designed. I'm fine, Mel. I take it you and the rest of your crew are okay?"

"Yeah, we're good— but we didn't take a direct hit from a bloody Cat Five. You're a lunatic, Rick Harvey. I'm not sure whether to kick you or kiss you."

Rick forced a laugh. "Maybe both? Next time we meet face to face, drinks are on me."

"Damn straight they are. No rush, though, now that I know you're still in one piece. Take your time, review your data. Send it on to Rosenstiel when you can." There was a long, staticky pause. "Was it worth it, Evel Knievel? Did you find any answers?"

"A few, Mel. For now, it's enough. I'll ring back when I can."

Rick ended the call. He took another longing look at his shrine, wandered over to the futon couch, and replayed the audio clip. This time, he heard the whispers differently; two voices speaking separately, then merging into one.

"Help, Rick."

"Help, Daddy."

"Help them."

The spirits of his wife and daughter reached out, awakened by the tempest, to help him cope. They lent him strength, purpose. Rick reached out with science to aid nameless, faceless people around the globe, vulnerable souls in coastal cities who lay in harm's way. His Hobbit House, or something like it, could help. If he refined the engineering, brought the costs down and made it cheaper to mass-produce, it could save lives. That was why Marta and Shannon still rode the storms: they didn't want him to surrender. Saving other families wouldn't bring them back. But it would honor their memories.

For that, Rick Harvey would ride a hundred hurricanes.

He sat there, alone and not alone, repeating the audio over and over while saltwater streamed down his stubbled cheeks. Wondering how many other ghosts sang inside the whirlwind, sharing secret messages of loss and hope. He would listen. He would tease their spirits out of the chaos to guide his path, to help him finish what he'd started.

Only when the whispers faded would he–and they–know peace.

C.E. WAGNER

United States

C.E. Wagner lives with her son and partner on the outskirts of Bloomington, IN, near the Hoosier National Forest, where she hikes and enjoys creek stomping. She has spent her life working in libraries and teaching Language Arts to secondary school students. After teaching for eleven years, she now works in a library again. When she was younger she lived in the woods for twelve years, thriving and learning a lot living an agrarian lifestyle without amenities like running water. She has been writing for as long as she can remember.

The idea for the novel *Repurpose* came to Wagner in 2015, when one morning it was raining so hard she wondered if driving to work was worth the risk. Wagner texted the first few sentences to herself while camping in Yellowstone. The rest of the novel came slowly over the next year while she worked as a receptionist. Wagner believes that to solve climate change we need to put forth narratives that explore real solutions rather than merely presenting dystopian stories; *Repurpose* presents one of these possible solutions.

REPURPOSE

a novel excerpt

Chapter 1: Wesley

He opened the letter alone. While his mother was still at work and his grandpa was out in the barn, Wesley Langbrook opened his Civil Service placement letter alone. He used the morning's butter knife, encrusted with bits of bread and butter he and his mother had made. His shaky fingers, still wet from walking in the unyielding rain, pried the adhesive away. The lip of the red, white, and blue envelope gave. The folded piece of paper stared at him, smooth and dangerous.

Wesley kicked his muddy boots off toward the back door of the kitchen. He pulled the letter out, feeling its slight weight. His heart beat noticeably in his chest. Then, he just opened it. The page was full of words that blurred together. Wesley focused his eyes on the first lines: *The United States of America orders Wesley James Langbrook to report for induction into the Civil Service Corp as of*–Wesley scanned down the page, looking for just the placement. Where was he going?

His wondering eyes snagged the word, but they went right over it. No, his brain said, disbelieving. His eyes settled on the place: Florida. "Yes!" he yelled, thrusting his fist into the air. Florida! He was going to one of the original cadet camps. He was going to see firsthand what true transformation could manifest.

He danced around the kitchen. "Thank you, God!" he sang a few times. Finally, he allowed the nearest chair to take his weight. Holding the paper with reverence, he thought back through the news vids of Stoneman Douglas being built and parts of Florida being lifted up out of water, solarized, desalinated, and sanitized. They even had an older woman there who had survived the shooting in Parkland at Marjory Stoneman Douglas High School. The camp and all the cadet camps to follow stood for social justice and change. Wesley felt gratitude rock his body. He had asked for this placement, and he had gotten what he prayed for.

He sat back and remembered the day the southern part of Florida disappeared. He had been eleven. His eleven-year-old self stopped wanting to play baseball and videos, and woke up into thinking and reflecting and observing. That day, the day of the Great Caribbean Earthquake, was the day Wesley truly understood in his gut that the world was changing.

The Great Caribbean Earthquake remade the land and sea. For the first time Wesley understood the globe was changing under his feet. Before that, it was simply violent storms and a Sunday-school prayer: "Take care of our planet; calm Mother Earth." When the Great Caribbean Earthquake and following tsunami consumed 25 percent of the Florida coastline and much of the remaining islands in the Caribbean in one evening, he felt fascinated and scared. How could cities, islands, and people just disappear into the ocean?

The Great Caribbean Earthquake happened on Thanksgiving. The Langbrook clan, what was left, clustered at Grandpa's house, an old farmhouse built in the early 20th century, in southern Indiana. It smelled musty until Grandpa's cooking permeated the house. He knew how to cook meat and potatoes for a feast. Though the family prided itself on storing food for winter, the best cut meat and most tender and unblemished vegetables were served.

Looking back, Wesley saw himself that morning. He stood in the living room in a worn pair of baseball pajama bottoms and his favorite blue sweater, watching the Flat on the wall. A few helicopters managed to film some of the tragedy as Puerto Rico and the Virgin Islands sank into the ocean simultaneously. Wesley watched the unreal footage as they showed it over and over again. Horrified, his mother told him to stop watching the news. In 3-D–the lands sinking into angry waters, waves taller than he had ever imaged rolling over coastline–was overwhelming and sublime. He was transfixed. She switched it to 2-D and resized the picture from ninety inches to forty, but even that was too horrible for her.

"Wesley, I don't want you watching that!" She grabbed his right hand and pulled as if to move him from the living room. "There's a reason it's only allowed on for four hours a day!" she yelled.

"Mom! Let go of me!" He pulled his hand free, and turned to face her. She was thin and her dark eyes flushed with worry. "Why can't I see what's really going on in the world?"

"I don't want you to worry or to be frightened," she said, grabbing him again.

"But mom, you're the one that's worried. You're the one who's frightened. If you protect me from everything that's bad, how can I ever fix it?"

She dropped his arm. "Fix it?" she questioned.

Wesley nodded. "Yeah. Aren't I supposed to fix it? That's what they tell us at church and school. My generation is going to fix it."

"That's an awfully tall order," she said, wide-eyed. Her dark forehead creased.

"Well, not me alone. I can't fix it alone, but I can do a little." He turned their attention back to the commotion on the Flat. He pointed to the buildings descending into water, disintegrating right as they hit. "If I don't know what's wrong, I can't help." He patted his mother's hand, now, like an adult would a child, and they sat down and watched the news unfold for an hour or so before Grandpa called them in to help clean up the morning's dishes. All the while, the smell of turkey twined about the rooms of the house.

~»

Later during dinner, Wesley remembered his grandpa talking about the weather, his nasally voice whistling as he drew out the words. "When I was a little boy," Grandpa started. He scooped a dome of white hot mashed potatoes on his plate, and continued, "people used to vacation in the Caribbean. They'd cruise on big luxury ships visiting the shores of pristine beaches." The old man was broad shouldered and tall. His thinning grey hair was pulled back in a wispy ponytail. He moved on to the broccoli.

"Dad, remember those are the last of our broccoli for a while," Wesley's mom reminded him.

He forked a slice of white meat and winked at Wesley's cousin Jennifer, who looked shy about eating the turkey she had named 'Trey.' "Big hurricanes kept hitting them until there was no reason to even try to rebuild." Grandpa went for the green beans next. He loved to eat and cook what he harvested, whether it was animal or vegetable. "It's a shame. Islands all over the world were the first to experience sea level rise. Couple that with erratic weather and strong storms–well, you know the result." He looked around the table. A gloom hung over them. The Caribbean islands just sunk into the ocean and Florida was forever impacted.

Wesley's mother and his dad's brother, Uncle David, began

eating. Jennifer and Wesley did too. Aunt Rachel smiled while Grandpa took a bite. "Mmmm—" the old man savored. "When I reached my twenties, dear Wesley," he said, his big eyes all on the child. Wesley thought his grandpa talked too much sometimes, but weather was captivating.

"I was a great gardener with your grandmother–God bless her soul. I kept a record of the weather. It really started getting crazy. According to my dad, the weather was dependable in the 20th century, regular, always in pattern. By the time I started keeping records, there were a lot of hurricanes, tornadoes, floods, fires—" He gesticulated with his fork.

"Some winters would be mild and then we'd get mountains of the fluffy stuff." He was buttering his roll; Wesley remembered his mother paid a good deal of money for the flour. "Summers could be in the 70s or in the 100s or jump back and forth. It just depended on what was happening with the jet stream or oceans." He took a bite of the roll. The butter dribbled a bit down his chin.

"It was below zero for almost two months this winter," Wesley said, starting to catch on. "That's not normal?" The meat tasted fleshy in his mouth until he mixed it with the broccoli and cranberries. He much preferred venison. When his father was alive, they killed at least one deer for the family every year.

"Yes, Wesley," Grandpa replied. "Now, it snows whenever it wants to and gets colder than a well digger's ass."

"Norman!" Wesley's mom said. Wesley's mom, in her prim dress, pushed her silky black hair behind her ears. "Norman, we've heard enough about the dire state of the weather."

"No!" Wesley said emphatically. "I want to know what it was like before!" He came up off his seat, and sat down. "Is it true that there were no Weather Days? Did your school ever get called off?" Aruna, his mother, looked at him. She frowned.

Sipping his water, Grandpa grinned. "We had what were called snow days, days off when the snow was bad, but nothing like you have today–only a few or even none a year. We never had days called off for floods or fog or torrential rain."

"Don't forget the tornado warnings!" Jennifer added with spunk.

"Weather Days started when your mom and dad and I were in high school," Uncle David explained. Like Wesley and his father, Uncle David's green eyes almost glowed. His hair was wavy like Wesley's, and his cheekbones lifted his bright eyes practically off his face. They inherited their eyes and from Wesley's grandmother, who passed away from lung cancer when the boy was just a toddler.

"Weather Days make it impossible to see my friends," said Jennifer. She only ate her beans and roll. She favored her mother in complexion. Wesley loved their walnut colored skin, and often wished he were darker complected like them or his own mother, whose mother and father were born of immigrants from Mumbai, India, fleeing from flooding begun decades ago.

"In some states they've completely gone over to classes online," Aunt Rachel pointed out. She pointed at her daughter's small plate of food. "Jennifer, kids are starving in Los Angeles and Chicago, so eat up. We don't let food go to waste."

"That's where we're all headed–distance learning," Uncle David joined in. "Thanks to the latest satellites. Should have been done long ago."

"I'm feeling like it's time for gratitude?" Wesley's mom, forever the noncontroversial one, said. "It is, after all, our nation's day of gratitude."

"When I was young, they still pretended it was about the Indians and Pilgrims sitting down together and havin' meal," Grandpa laughed. "Now, everyone says it's about thanks, pretending the Native American genocide never happened."

"We know, dad," Aruna sighed. She was obviously aggravated with Grandpa. Wesley thought it was funny. Grandpa was just telling the truth. His mom wished all conflict away.

"I am grateful for you, my family," Grandpa started. "You're the rock I sit on."

They toasted each other with bartered grape juice and went around the table sharing little notes of thanks.

~»

Wesley had been so captivated with the weather that particular Thanksgiving, and now, as a teenager, it was a nuisance, a buzzing fly that Wesley was determined to fix. It disrupted electrical services, dropped trees on stores and houses. How could you keep vehicles on the streets when the streets were sinking? How could you have alternative energy like windmills when the weather knocked them over? They kept saying, "Plant more trees. Plant more trees. They're our lungs. We need more trees." But trees toppled just as much as windmills. Climate change was a frustrating opponent, and Wesley was tired of all the inconveniences it posed. Like today! Another Weather Day. Another day separated from Corey, Adam, and Lisa due to torrential downpours crumbling buildings and roads. Another day full of high winds and hail targeting trees and houses. Another day spent online in class discussion in the cyber classroom; that is, if signal was even working. Was college going to be like this? Would college even exist when he got out of Civil Service? Regardless, he was determined to do his part to better the world. He touched the class icon on the Flat his mobile projected and made sure the audio pickup was on. "Wesley here."

"Ah, Mr. Langbrook! Thanks for joining us!" Mr. Teague, Wesley's US History teacher said. The man was dignified and engaging. He had winning eyes, and, this morning, a baseball cap and pajamas on. One of Wesley's favorite teachers ever, Mr. Teague made him laugh and, perhaps more importantly, made Wesley see things in a different way. Mr. Teague continued, "Today we're discussing our Civil Service placements since graduation is staring us in the face." He looked away from his camera for a second. "Did you get your placement yet, Wesley?"

"Yes!" Wesley said enthusiastically. Being a history buff, he loved talking about the War on Terrorism or the Civil Rights Movements or the Warren/Kroskrity Antitrust Laws that were ending run-away capitalism, but today the future began. On his Selective Service application, he had put his interests down as "water conservation" and "engineering" and "architecture." Since they implemented Civil Service three years ago, it seemed like most kids ended up cleaning sewers, fixing broken bridges, or converting the millions of miles of disintegrating roads into rail lines. He didn't want to spend time repairing the infrastructure people decades before ignored. He had requested to be sent to Stoneman Douglas, the closest of the original five camps. Most kids from Karstburg seemed to be getting sent out West or up the East Coast. Corey and he joked they were going to end up at Yellowstone when it blew, destroying all the railways and bridges their classmates fixed.

"Well?" Mr. Teague said, bringing Wesley back from his interior thoughts.

"I've been stationed in Florida," he said.

Several small heads stopped bobbing on their tiny replicas on the bottom of the Flat. Adam yelled, "What! What kind of pilin' crap is that?" He was the dirty blond in the screen box in the middle.

"You'll be pilin' that's for sure!" someone blurted out. They'd all seen plenty of news vids of people piling things after floods, tornados, and other natural disasters. Some of them had done some pilin' themselves.

"Enough from you all," Mr. Teague said. "Let's go around clockwise and just say where your assignment is. No one else comment," Mr. Teague directed. "Jamie, you start."

Jamie said, "Cheyenne, Wyoming."

Adam, one of Wesley's oldest friends, said, "Devens, Massachusetts." Wesley's heart fell into his stomach. Massachusetts? They were supposed to be together.

Someone said, "Richmond, Kentucky" and another person said, "Cheyenne like Jamie."

Then it was Corey's turn. Corey, Adam, and Wesley had been friends since elementary school. Even though he knew his placement last night, Wesley didn't dare tell them. As long as he didn't share, he could daydream the placements would be the same. Maybe Corey would get Florida, too; then they could petition to get Adam's assignment changed. Wesley looked hopeful, but Corey said, "Prince George, Virginia." He looked at Wesley apologetically as if it was his fault. Adam put his head down on his desk, and the rotation continued on: someone was going to Maine, two to California, another to Kentucky, Wesley was the only one going to Florida, three more to Wyoming, Lisa ended up with Tennessee, and the last was going to Alaska.

Mr. Teague leaned forward, pushing his ball cap's bill down. "I know you have a lot to say. You're not happy. No one ever is. You're cursing the Paperless Act of 2026, wishing all snail mail had been eradicated. You're pouting, thinking the government is going to ruin your life." He sat back. "It's changing, folks. Karstburg is no longer your little shelter from the rest of the world. We're going to watch some vids from former grads who've been where you are right now, but first, I want you to jot down some of your thoughts."

Wesley tapped his mobile, grumbling with many of his classmates. The Flat went from 3-D to a 2-D writing surface. His friends disappeared while he typed pointedly.

I'm going to Stoneman Douglas in Florida! This is what I have wanted—to help build a new society, a new city. I have questions: How many people live there now? Will I help with evacuations? Oh, it says that I'll be "restoring and rejuvenating the ocean." I hope they don't have any of those waterborne diseases or bacteria that eat your skin. I'm going to spend the next two years of my life cleaning up the line between ocean and civilization! When's the last time I even went swimming? I'll need to practice! I'm excited and scared all wrapped up into one. Will it be dangerous? Will it be fun?

Wesley stared at the word dangerous and then fun. He couldn't think of anything else to write. Everything felt surreal. Tapping and flipping the Flat again, he could see his classmates were done.

Everyone sat in silence. Mr. Teague finally broke the tension. "Well, they certainly have placed you all over this year." He smiled encouragingly. "Who wants to share first?"

*

Chapter 2: Nora

The sidewalk, in the sunlight, looked stone white, flecked with red. Wisps of the last brown grass scuttled across it in the afternoon breeze. At least there was a breeze. These days a "breeze" was a rare event. I heard two different kinds of insects. Despite the unrelenting heat, life kept on even if "life" meant ravenous insects consuming every organic thing in sight. The flag's grommets and cord hit the school's flagpole. In the distance, I could hear someone running a motor. The sky was blue, devoid of clouds; just blue. I walked through the parking lot breathing my stinking saliva through my red bandana, my tennis shoes softening into the steaming hot pavement, sticky and glue-like. The sun glowered, making my skin moisten. The light red hairs on my arm glowed, and my sweat smelled like overheated peanut butter.

I walked onto the road, a dusty red thing of a path, and headed toward the only convenience store for miles. We, what's left of my town, call it Belinda's. I peered in the main window before opening the door. The bell rang as I opened it, announcing my presence. I walked across the old, shabby wooden floor to the counter, listening to the old boards groan. The store smelled like quinoa muffins and last week's fruit dehydrated by heated sand.

"What will it be today, Nora?" a squat woman asked me. Her blue eyes were small and being wrinkled by the folds of her excess, freckled skin. Her smile held onto a worn-out hope. Her hands were rugged. Oftentimes, I saw myself in her—the freckles, the strawberry blonde hair, the solid small frame. We both looked great in our cowboy hats.

"I'd like an oatmeal cookie, Gran." I slipped my forest green backpack on the floor.

"That would be a wonderful thing," she said. Sugar and oats were nearly impossible to get; chocolate had disappeared long ago. I remembered making real oatmeal cookies with Belinda when I was very small. As the years went by, we substituted other ingredients: applesauce for oil and butter, honey for sugar, and old nutmeg for cinnamon.

She coughed, waking me from my oatmeal reverie. "How was school?"

I took a bite of the bland muffin she offered me before answering, weighing my words. "Well, they couldn't get the 'robots' connected until after ten. Mr. Lopez is getting crankier." Gran shook her head knowingly, and I ate a few bites of my muffin, watching her stifle a cough. "Another kid, Joey, didn't show up today. That leaves fourteen of us in the senior class." I swallowed a bit of water Gran offered. I noticed it had a few grains of sand in it. "We started the year out with fifty-four, Gran, fifty-four."

"It's a might bit scary, isn't it, Nora?" she whispered.

I nodded, looking out at the deserted streets and the landscape beyond. Tennponey had always been small, just a note on the musical score of the high desert, but now everyone was leaving. Rumor had it the Feds wanted people to leave, but the state put laws in place to discourage migrating to other states; they wanted to make sure people had "safe" places to go before leaving; some said the state needed the population numbers for federal revenue. People were fleeing the Southwest in droves before they enacted their law. Who wanted to live where there was no longer water? Even the mountains above Tennponey were turning to stone and sand. Year after year less snow was falling, and the snowpack was getting smaller. Fires destroyed what forests were left in the mountains, and then insects finished them off. Everything was blowing away in one big continuous sandstorm.

I remembered Gran. I had to get her someplace safer, someplace without sand and dust. "I wish," I started, "we could just run away North together. Maybe we could sneak into Canada," I joked. I wanted things to be like they were when I was little, when grass still grew and the cattle still roamed our ranch.

"Nora, you know what we're going to do." She patted my hand. "You're going to finish school, and while you're doing your two-year Civil Service, you'll find some nice midwestern boy to marry, so we can move out of this sandbox." Gran smiled innocently, and then coughed.

"I'm not going to leave you!" I raised my voice. "And I am not going to just marry some guy to get residency in some swamp land like Ohio or Kentucky!" I squeezed her hand. "Besides, I like girls." I winked at Gran. She smiled back and pretended to push me off the chair.

"You're hopeless, Nora. You haven't even dated anyone."

"Well, it's hard to date when everyone's covered in bandanas to keep the sand out. They all look the same, boys and girls alike."

Gran laughed her full-hearted laugh, which turned into cough. Of course. I handed her the glass of water between us and watched while she gathered her breath. Then, she stood up straight and looked me in the eye. "You should be wearing your breathing mask, not that damned bandana."

"All the kids, all fourteen of us, wear bandanas." I took another muffin bite.

I guess Gran was feeling a bit ruthless, because she dropped a blunt sandwich next. "I've decided to file bankruptcy and go to Farmington."

"No! You can't leave!" I yelled. "Who will keep the store up?" My heart beat fast. We had talked about this before, argued about it, and I always thought I had talked her out of it.

She grabbed my hand. "Nora, I can't keep the store up. Another refrigerator went down today. Mr. Gunderson at the bank had a long talk with me today. The town is dead, dear. That's the pure truth of it."

"But Pawpa's dad and grandfather built this store! The ranch is practically unlivable. How can we let this go too?" In my mind it came down to this: we were the life and blood of Tennponey. We just could not abandon the place. Our family had been here since 1874.

My grandmother slammed her fist down on the counter. "We never belonged here!" she said. It rang in my ears. Her body collapsed in defeat, coughing.

I dropped to the floor, hugging her until her cough subsided. "Our ancestors are from England for Christ sakes." She looked so tired. "The sand is reclaiming it, Nora. It's time to leave when you graduate in May. That's final. I won't talk about it anymore." With that she lifted herself up, walked away, resuming her coughing.

I threw what was left of the muffin against the wall and pouted. In less than two months, I'd be sent off somewhere for my Civil Service duty, and I'd never see Tennponey again.

~»

The day after graduation, Gran and I took an e'bus to Farmington after handing the keys to the store over to Mr. Gunderson. The bus was full of dust and families leaving for better opportunities. Even though I heard on the news we were "climate refugees," I couldn't apply that to myself or my Gran. It was somehow like admitting defeat, and I could not, would not ever do that. I had been through too much in my eighteen years. I refused to give in, to give up. Somehow, I would make a respectable life for my grandmother and myself. No matter what. I would do it. So, the government was sending me to Florida. Maybe I could make some connections there, or somehow get stationed closer to home. Last year when we had to fill out the forms about our placement, I was so pissed off I had put "Anywhere, USA" as my first choice. I think my second choice was something like "FU, UF." I thought it was funny, made me feel better for a second, but now it's gotten me a ticket to Florida. At least it's South. I was used to being hot. I had put down I was interested in marine biology as a joke. I didn't even know how to swim!

More people got on the bus and more e'cars and pods showed up on the highway the closer we got to Farmington. People entered the bus with dust in their hair and scarves, and masks of every color over their mouths and faces. There were dark people with dark eyes, people with brown skin and cynical eyes, and there were light people with sunburns and eyes the color of skies without rain. Mostly, there were people the color of creamed coffee looking out of bloodshot eyes, stinging from lack of rain. They wore discouragement on their backs and carried suitcases and backpacks full of empty dreams. With its computerized voice, the bus told us to sit back and enjoy the ride, but we all sat silently, watching the desert go by, turning the mountains turn to dust, rock by rock.

When we hit Albuquerque, the air felt a little more breathable. I noticed color off the road, bits of pale green among the white rocks and mountains. And then there was the city with the Central Plaza towering over the streets, and the newer, even taller Sandia Trust Building. Buildings were covered with vertical gardens and solar panels. Huge windmills spread out across the horizon.

I couldn't see the Rio Grande from the bus, but I could feel it. The river was water; it was life, and even though the city managed the water well, the daily ins and outs of a shrinking water supply filled the news. Green burst out of the landscape like a big flower. It made me thirsty for some reason, and some woman broke open an orange and handed slices to people around her. An orange! How did she get an orange? We pulled into the Alvarado Transportation Center to disembark and gather up more passengers.

Gran interrupted my thoughts on water. "Do you remember when you were little and your mom and dad took you to the BioPark Aquarium and Botanical Garden?"

She caught me off guard. I turned from the window to look at her. Belinda Evans looked older than her 58 years. How old did I look? I didn't want my brain to think about my mom and dad. Gran looked away in sorrow, and immediately I felt guilty. I squeezed her hand and said softly, "Of course I do." She squeezed back, and then the robot voice called out that we were departing the station.

We remained quiet for a long time. The sun was creeping out overhead, baking the bus, demanding everything from its air conditioner. With mountains and scrub on both sides, I couldn't help but wonder about my dad. I felt like I needed to break the silence, so I took a stab at it. "Do you ever wonder where he is?" I knew Gran would know who I was talking about, my dad, the last man standing, the broken man hiding.

The windows were dusty, but she slid over a bit and pointed up toward the Jemez Mountains. "I always imagine him up there, living on berries and bark, killing bears for food. I don't know. He could be dead for all we know." She sat back, fanning herself with her hand. "I'm still not over being mad at him for leaving you." She coughed.

"Gran, he was worthless," I said. "When mom died, he died. All he did was drink. If a bear got him, the poor beast would get drunk eating him." I remembered my dad at the kitchen table, refusing to eat dinner, simply drinking beer after beer. After hybrid trucks were taken off the road, and he lost his job, he switched to whiskey for dinner. Then, he was drunk every day when I came home from school. He'd want to talk to me, tell me how wonderful I was and how I looked just like my mom. His speech would get strange and slurry, and he'd hang on me, saying he loved me. But then, I'd do something and take my attention off of him, and the tirade would start. He'd tell me how useless I was, how I never did anything for him, and how disappointed my mom would have been in me. If Gran was around, she'd kick him out, but she wasn't always around. She had a store to run after all, and Pawpa Pete was running the ranch. One night when I was nine it got so bad, I ran away. I called the store from the school parking lot, and kept running as I was talking. Pawpa Pete chased dad out of town with an old shotgun. He chased his own son away. The Sheriff could have arrested Pawpa for carrying a shotgun in town, but they knew the situation. They stood back-up. We found out later dad had taken several of Pawpa's permitted hunting guns. We never heard from him again, except for one letter that said he was living with some survivalists. They would survive the environmental apocalypse and we wouldn't.

"He wasn't always hopeless, Nora," Gran interrupted. "He loved your mother and you very much before his mind went. He was responsible and loyal, even handsome. He was a good boy and a good man. His mind just snapped. A lot of people's minds have snapped with The Fall." She winked at me through a cough.

"Don't make excuses for him. He was a jerk. He couldn't handle mom's death. What he did was worse than die. He became a monster. He was supposed to be there," I caught my breath. I would not cry, I would not. "He wasn't there for me." Another breath. I steady myself. "He is dead to me." I let out a little air, holding back the tears. "I don't care to talk about the waste of oxygen he's been on this planet. I wish I could tear out the part of my chromosomes that came from him." My jaw held firm, my eyes narrowed, and I felt my frown sink deeper into my face. I hated that man.

Gran just nodded, knowingly. I had grown a wall of resentment toward him I made sure no one could ever breach. No one. I nurtured my hatred and it made me feel a whole lot better.

I left Gran in a train station in Farmington, New Mexico, with the hot, hot sun shining down like a sniper looking for targets. She was off to work in the sands, filling bags of the stuff for the places in the country flooding and sinking into water. Farmington was on the Trans-American Pipeline, which pumped excess rainwater from the Midwest to the West. Unlike a lot of southwestern towns dying from heat and the megadroughts, Farmington was having a revival. There were jobs in wind energy and construction. Getting a ticket out to a better place was peddled and possible. Of course, we hadn't signed up to be evacuated or to migrate. Pawpa Pete was too proud. He kept waiting for it to rain, for the cattle to come back to life, for the world to be new all over again. We left him in Tennponey, and he'd surely turn to dust before we saw him again. Gran's hope now rested with me. I was her ticket out if I could find another home. Problem was, I agreed with Pawpa Pete. I just wanted to blow away with all the sand. I'd rather be hot any day than cold or wet.

*

Chapter 3: Wesley

Once, the Langbrook farm had been picturesque. Wesley imagined it looked like those old fashioned Christmas cards with the perfectly weathered white farmhouse looking warm and inviting with just the right amount of Christmas wreaths on the doors complete with fake candle lights in each window. Too, the postcard would have a sleigh being pulled by horses with the moon overhead. Cows would be in the barn, and the people inside the house would be content and whole. Not like today where families had holes in them, holes made by disease and tragedies. Every kid Wesley knew was missing a parent or a sibling or both. Diseases like staph, asthma, and mycobacterium infections were killing a lot of people. It seemed like researchers were always on the verge of a cure for cancer, but it never happened.

Today, he was leaving home. Descending the stairs, he rubbed his hand down the old drywall. His mom and grandpa waited for him in the kitchen. What if he never came back from Florida? Even though the fences were always in need of mending, and the gardens struggled, and the goats got out too often, this was home. This drafty old farmhouse was his home. Running in the woods, stomping the creek, shoveling the snow—what would he be without these things to anchor him? He'd have to find new anchors, and of course, there was always his relationship with God.

His stocking feet reached the bottom stair. He looked into the kitchen. The white drapes with the tiny red and yellow flowers. The dish detergent on the sink with its lid open. The yellowed cabinets that needed fixing. He walked in. The chipped gray tile. His mom looked so beautiful in the morning light. She had his favorite shirt on: the Karstburg High Bulldogs. It was obvious she had been crying. Her tears made her dark eyes even more vivid. He held his arms out to her, and she dove into his embrace. Soon, he felt Grandpa holding them both.

"Thank you both for everything you've given me," Wesley said.

"Oops! I can't let the pancakes burn!" Grandpa disengaged, and they all collected themselves.

Wesley sat down on the middle chair, the one with the broken back piece. It was where he sat all his life. "I am going to miss you two more than you probably know," he said. His words sounded inadequate. He wondered how he could possibly sum up the importance of these two people, and his utter sadness at leaving them?

His mom handed him a glass of water with apple slices in it. "Without you, this house will seem

empty."

"It's time we rent out some rooms," Grandpa said, placing his famous potato pancakes in front of

Wesley. Unlike in some areas of the country, flour was somewhat easy to get in the Midwest.

"You should open a restaurant," Wesley replied. He'd been telling his grandpa that for years.

Grandpa served another stack. "I just might apply to be a cook down at Feldstein's if it ever opens again." Last fall, Feldstein's was hit by lightning and caught on fire.

Then, they made small talk, because big talk is sometimes too big for words. They went over the topics they frequented day after day: their lack of money and resources, mom's job at the school, what they can do with the farm, and their beloved church community. No one mentioned Wesley going to Florida for two years. No one mentioned the unknown. His mom taught him the art of denial, worry, and hope. He wished to wrap up the past and leave it behind. The farmhouse. What once was. He was ready for the crumbling world.

There was time for all three to clean up their dishes. He dried the last plate, and placed the tightly woven cotton towel to his nose. It smelled like fabric and love and family. Though he knew he would miss his childhood home, he felt more than ready to tackle the challenges ahead. He was going to make the world a better place.

~»

Upstairs he put on his boots and grabbed his worn blue duffel bag. He went to his dresser where his personal altar remained. He fingered an acorn his first girlfriend had given him on a walk, a special stone with a hole inside it, and lastly, a hawk feather he found two years ago. Then, he picked up the knife his dad had given him, held it to his breast, and whispered a prayer of thanks. He placed the knife down and left the room.

Outside of his bedroom door, standing in the narrow hall, he heard his mother sit down in her bedroom. The old wood floor creaked with exhaustion when her weight hit the bed. His dad had died in that bed. Outside, Wesley heard the wind pick up with the unrelenting rain.

About to walk downstairs, his feet were stayed by his mother's words. She was praying. "Dear Lord," she whispered, "let me be an instrument of your remaking of the world. Help me see gratitude in the damage we have done to Mother Earth and give me hope for the future." She paused. He leaned closer to her door.

"Especially for my son, especially for him and his generation. Look over him at Camp Stoneman Douglas. Blessed Be, Amen."

With a smile, Wesley started down the stairs. Outside the rain pebbled the farmhouse windows. The tree roots rotted in the cold, spring mud. The hooves of animals ached with disease from being wet. Gardens refused to grow. The sun remained hidden behind a gray-brown forest of clouds. Creeks swelled, roads sunk, and houses fell into disrepair. Black mold creeped into houses sideways and whispered choking secrets into lungs.

~»

Wesley had never ridden on a bullet train, or any train, before. He had wanted to take a solar flight from Indy, but air travel had been inconsistent since the torrential downpours started weeks ago. Mom and Grandpa drove him in a rented e'car to the train station after breakfast. They left each other with words of prayer and grace and hopes for a bright future.

The bullet train zipped through Kentucky, which looked just like Indiana. With his favorite number-two pencil, he drew trees melting into a creek. When he was finishing up the alarmed fish with big eyes, the landscape began to look different. Tennessee surrounded him. The Smokey Mountains were still green and covered in beautiful mist. It looked like an enchanted forest, except Wesley knew about the killer fog episodes and some tree die-offs from insects. Nothing was untouched by climate disruption these days. Birds were having a hard time finding food. They still migrated with the length of the day, but insects that they ate were hatching during different months due to warmer temperatures. Erratic storms raged. Lightning caused nonstop fires in the West. Water was scarce in some places and overly abundant in others, like Indiana. Luckily the government and private sector were working together on solutions. The

Trans-American Pipeline was a good example. Other parts of the world weren't so cooperative or lucky. War waged in the polar regions over water, fertile soil, and what little oil was left. During Wesley's Civil Service duty, military recruiters would be present, trying to get them to sign up to enforce and maintain civility in other parts of the world. A few kids from Karstburg had already signed up on the special direct path to the military; it would become part of their Civil Service duty. Wesley? He was not interested in bullying or shooting other people. Though to be fair, he did hear the military helped people, too. They did a lot of the things he would do in cadet school: build houses and levees, put out fires, help move climate refugees, and other do-good stuff. Wesley considered drawing muscular, military types with "do good stuff" tattooed on their biceps. He decided against it.

Tennessee gave way to Georgia. The light became blinding as the train barreled down into the foothills of the Appalachians. He saw a huge solar farm in the distance, people working on more arrays up near the I75 tracks. He couldn't help but smile at the sun; he had rarely seen it in the last year. Clouds seemed permanently sewn into the fabric of the Indiana sky. He took a picture of the blurred landscape and sent it to Corey and Adam. Corey was already in Virginia, and Adam wasn't leaving for Massachusetts for another week. Adam texted back, *SUN!!! I'm coming with you!* But Wesley didn't hear back from Corey. After he put his sketchbook away, Wesley bathed in the warm heat from the windows as he marveled at the metal and concrete called "Atlanta." It seemed unreal as it stretched toward the heavens, soaking up sunshine with millions of reflective surfaces. Atlanta was well-known for its innovative energy designs. He wondered how many kilowatts were being generated this very morning. How many were being sent out to places like Karstburg, which had little hopes of solar generation?

The train came to a stop at a Trans-Coastal station in Atlanta. According to Wesley's ticket instructions, he'd be getting on a new train here. With excitement and little trepidation, he grabbed his duffel bag and backpack, and moved to the exit.

Chapter 4: Nora

As the train pulled into Tate Bay, where Camp Stoneman Douglas was located, I woke up from dreaming I was drowning in a sandstorm, coughing and suffocating on particles of red dust. The rose sun heated up my face, beating through the window. It was low on the horizon. Late afternoon was inviting the touch of early evening. Wispy looking pines and thick-trunked trees like I saw growing farther North dotted yards. These were similar to the ones I saw growing in Missouri and Tennessee, but with a lot more space between their leaves. It was like a god had come down from the heavens and told the trees their branches couldn't be too close together. It looked kind of odd. There were palm trees, too. I recognized them from all the hurricane vids I had seen on the news.

I sat up more in my blue seat, taking in the town. It looked more like the Southwest than I expected. A lot of buildings were pink, tan, and beige–the colors of the desert. Solar panels were on most of the roofs, and the whitewashed streets and paths were accented with photovoltaics embedded in the knee-high lamps, benches, and even the ground. Many of the buildings had brightly colored frills and banners hanging. One read, *Welcome Civil Service Cadets!* Really? There were even some festive, huge yellow flowers blooming. I was imagining dirty pink flamingoes, turned-over old-time cars with seaweed, and the incoherent poor pushing old grocery carts around. The place actually looked cheery.

I waited until the mass of young people gossiped and giggled their way off the train compartment. No one had sat next to me. I wasn't what you call "welcoming." When all the silly cadets had left and all was quiet, I stood up and grabbed my bag off of the top rack. My tennis shoes still held the New Mexico sand in between the dirty, beige laces. I bent down as if to tie a shoe, but instead, I moistened my finger, pressed some sand into it, and brought the desert to my mouth. It was who I was. I wouldn't forget.

The main building looked like a renovated hotel, a tan stucco affair with a huge arch out front blocking some of the glare from hundreds of identical windows. No doubt that was the dormitory. Someone had carved *Camp Stoneman Douglas, Home Base* on the arch. When I pulled the door open I was blasted with cooler air and a noisy line of the cadets. I guessed I wasn't going to escape them anytime soon. I pulled out my mobile, a ragged old tab with a broken screen. I had texted Gran several times over the last sixteen hours, but had gotten no reply. I typed *I have arrived. More later. Love, Nora* and sent it off, hoping the weather was good enough between here and New Mexico to carry my information. You just never knew these days. Towers, buildings, water pipes, windmills—whatever was built could be blown down. Wind and erosion seemed to be winning at the current game of development. We'd be back in the pretechnological era if it wasn't for all the satellites.

When I finally reached the overly veneered front desk, a tired looking woman gave me a look that said, "Finally, the last one." She had on a uniform of smart crease lines and drab olive. Dutifully, she put on her smile and gave me the routine. I was to go up to my room—she handed me a key card with the number 238 on it with instructions to download the app—unpack, freshen up, and be back downstairs in the Grand Hall—she pointed to my right and I could see double doors opened to a large room—by 6:00 p.m. (EST). She made sure I had a mobile. When she saw my screen was cracked, she offered me a free, government issue. I declined, but thought I might reconsider very soon. I thanked her and headed toward the salmon colored door marked "stairs."

A tall girl with jet black hair was occupying room 238. She'd left the door open and was parading around opening drawers and depositing items in them. Obviously, she had taken the north side of the room. Hesitantly, I walked in, eyeing her perfect jeans and bright shirt. She wore a few bracelets and had fancy barrettes in her hair. She seemed to be humming and kind of dancing around. When my elk-hide bag hit my bed, she stopped, her hands frozen with a hairbrush and fancy pins. I managed a guttural and awkward, "Hi!" Then, I remembered I should probably introduce myself. "I'm Nora Evans. I'm from New Mexico."

Quite the performer, she put her hand with the fancy hair pins over her mouth, then down, then back over her mouth like she was super stunned. Yes, people do still live in the Southwest, stupid, I wanted to say. "I'm Makaleigh Garcia from the Granite state, New Hampshire." She put her hair tools down on her bed, and stepped up to shake my hand. I returned the gesture. It was pleasant enough.

"Isn't this exciting? I'm from Lincoln. I went to a boarding school up in the mountains, St. Ann's. What's it like in New Mexico?" I didn't think Makaleigh took a breath while she talked, and she almost squealed with delight. She was like Miss Privilege on cheerleading steroids–just the kind of girl I would have liked to have hated if I had had a normal teenage experience, which I didn't.

"Ah," I said real slow in response. "Northern New Mexico is fairly normal except for all the climate refugees. The southern part of the state has turned into a full out desert. There's nothing much left but sand." I opened my bag and started pulling out my purple toothbrush, black hair brush, underwear, and clothes. Compared to Makaleigh, I had very little.

"I'm so sorry," she bounced.

Froufrou is the word that came to my mind. I really disliked fluffy girls. They give the rest of us a bad name. "Has New Hampshire lost a lot of coastline?" I asked, trying to make conversation while opening my allotment of drawers in the room.

"Actually," her voice flounced in a sing-song manner, "a lot of folks don't know this, but New Hampshire has hardly any coastline. We're bordered on either side by Massachusetts and Maine, and yes, there has been some coastal loss, but we're bouncing back quite well compared to other New England states. It's affecting our mountains, though. We've had our share of fires. And oh! oh!" Her face went through a range of emotions. "The insects have hurt our maple trees. That's why you find it hard to get any good maple syrup these days." She flounced.

"I don't think I've ever had real maple syrup," I said, turning back to my modest pile of shirts.

"I'll have to get you some!" She was putting away one teal suitcase and beginning on another.

We put our things away in awkward silence. Inside my head, I was complaining loudly about having been placed in a room with a shallow, empty-headed doll. How in the hell was this going to work? I just wanted to beat something.

"I'm nervous," Makaleigh piped up after a minute or two. She sat down on her newly made bed, and looked right at me. Her dark eyes took in the light and shined. Somehow, they reminded me of chocolate chips, which made me think of Gran's cookies from long ago. I looked away. "I've never been away from home or school," she continued. "My parents never let me go on church or community mission trips to help people in disaster areas. This is all new to me," she confessed. "I can't imagine what it would be like to lose my home."

"Try losing your whole town, practically your whole state," I mumbled. I twisted my favorite plaid shirt in my hands. "I don't want to be a downer, but I'm not real happy about being here."

Makaleigh shook her head. Her mobile beeped, and she took it up with enthusiasm, squealing the words, "Mom and Dad!" I went to the bathroom, astonished at the lack of sand in the pristine, white shower.

~»

The Grand Hall was overwhelmingly full of young people, chatting and laughing. Together, the sound of their voices roared in my ears, making me want to leave the room immediately. I was in line behind an awkward boy with big ears; he looked fifteen instead of eighteen or nineteen. The walls around me were a faded green. Light came in from a huge greenhouse attached to the room. It was full of plants with big leaves of every shade of green. Sun tubes from the greenhouse brought in the waning evening light.

Unfortunately, there was a table equipped with military types taking names and handing out badges, and sadly, directing cadets to certain tables. A nice looking man with a stern smile and straight lips asked me my name. He dutifully found me on his screen, and wrote my name on a badge. He grabbed a packet of materials, wrote an email address on the top, and finally looked up at me. He stopped a moment. "You're in the Chokoloskee cohort, over there." He pointed to a table near the front and right side. I was thinking, "The what?" as I walked slowly away from the military types to my table.

Looking at all the occupied seats, it was obvious I was the last to arrive. Conveniently, Makaleigh was several spaces down from the empty seat. She was chatting with a blond who looked too tan to be completely white, as they used to say. Most of the heads of hair at the table were dark. Some were curly. There seemed to be an even number of males to females. As I sat down, most eyes took me in. Most people do when you have strawberry blond hair like some ancient Irish wench. I smiled sarcastically, and physically moved my chair so I could see the podium, turning my back on the majority of my cohort. Cohort–what an obnoxious word. *Junkin' star shit, what had I gotten myself into?*

*

Chapter 5: Wesley

Wesley was relieved to sit down in the conference hall. Finally, he would be told what was going on, what to expect, and Grafton, his new roommate, could talk to someone else. Grafton put Wesley on edge. Wesley looked forward to the dimming of the lights. Looking around, he marveled at the sun tubes, giant tropical-looking plants, and the LED cluster lamps. He could get pumped about learning about alternative energies and salvaging half-submerged cities. More and more young people filed in all around him. Lastly, a redhead stormed up to the table, grabbed the last chair, and promptly turned it around. The lights went off and curtains were pulled, blocking the sun streaming into the side greenhouse.

"Salvage, Repurpose, Rebuild, and Survive," a deep voice boomed across the room. Two screens filled with pictures of machines pulling twisted houses, cars, and furniture out of flooded streets. Then, the screens filled with young people constructing buildings, using machinery, manufacturing solar panels, and discussing things with engineering types.

A man came into view behind a podium in the middle. He spoke the words again, "Salvage, Repurpose, Rebuild, and Survive. I'm Raphael Cruz, the director of Camp Stoneman Douglas. I want to welcome you all here to our main headquarters. The next two years of your lives will be electrifying. You will find a career. You will help restore beaches, wetlands, and communities. You will build the future. You will learn skills to use in the creation of a new United States. You are the future. You are here to save the world. We here at Stoneman Douglas will equip you with the tools to do just that. But you, yes you, are the most valuable tool of all. It is your ideas that will shape the future."

Grafton leaned in and whispered in Wesley's ear, "We're superheroes!"

"Salvage, Repurpose, Rebuild, and Survive. It's our motto. I believe in it so deeply, I have it tattooed on my arm." Mr. Cruz, the spotlight now on him, flexed his bicep, showing his tattoo. He grinned with his small mouth, topped with a brushy mustache. Wesley burst into applause.

The screens began showing a short documentary about the history of the Civil Service Corps, featuring ancient footage from the 1940s and President Franklin's New Deal. It detailed how the idea came from over one hundred years ago with FDR's Civil Works Administration and other organizations that pulled the country out of the Great Depression. It described how many countries throughout the centuries had required young people to devote time to improving life for their fellow citizens. The film continued on explaining how Congress had enacted the Civil Service Corps just three years earlier, piggybacking off of the Selective Service. Next, the film showed many of the projects the Civil Service Corps had accomplished in those three short years: miles of coastal waters planted in marsh trees and plants, levees built, roads converted to rail, flooded cities salvaged for wood and metal, garbage dumps mined for resources, solar collectors erected, bladeless and regular windmills built and placed, and wave energy generators constructed and floated out on the ocean.

"I lived through the Caribbean Earthquake, tsunami, and coastal loss. I lived in Southern Florida and was rescued from our roof. My family lost everything. I was a young man of sixteen, and I was resilient. My parents and many other adults weren't so lucky. They succumbed to depression and grief. They had a difficult time adapting. Young people are naturally adaptable and full of dreams. They are innovative and creative. It's your imagination, yes, your imagination that has the power to change the world. Not just the United States, but the entire world."

"This man is goofy," Grafton murmured in Wesley's ear. Trying to look a little disapproving, Wesley gave him a squinted look.

Mr. Cruz continued, "We have the power to clean up and change our ways. Salvage, Repurpose, Rebuild, and Survive. We're going to do much better than survive. We are going to thrive!" Many in the audience cheered along with Wesley.

The screens started showing pictures of a green and blue landscape, a place where water and land lived together. Wesley recognized it as the lost Florida Everglades.

"In a sense, this camp is named after the brave students of Marjory Stoneman Douglas High School from the early part of this century. Certainly, their passion to change what was wrong and improve society is something we long to capture and cultivate. But this camp is also named after Marjory Stoneman Douglas herself, the famous journalist who championed the Everglades. Even though she lived in the early 1900s, she recognized the importance of the Everglades' ecosystem to the health of the state. She fought against the destruction of wetlands and the natural systems of protection from the ocean." Mr. Cruz paused and allowed the pictures of the once glorious marshlands to be viewed. Pictures of trees entwined, creating an arch in the water, blue herons and other birds Wesley didn't recognize alighted on water, and many pictures of the sinuous paths of water embroidering green, green land. It was enchanting to look at.

"Each of you is in a cohort named after a place in the Everglades: places like Big Cypress, Flamingo, Chokoloskee, and Long Sound. The people who came before, the people who made their lives in these towns and cities and fishing holes loved the land that is now underwater. It is human nature to love where we live. Right now, we are on the cusp of great opportunity. We have the ability and desire to help Mother Nature reshape our landscapes and create a future where weather, nature, and all living beings can live in harmony. You sit there quietly, but I encourage you to not be quiet. Be loud. Be an architect of our future!"

Wesley had already been primed by church and school for such speeches. He accepted the duty; his generation was here to reinvent living on earth, incorporating habits long abandoned with new technologies. His mother made sure he knew his sustainability principles. He understood mass marketing revolved around motivating young people toward a future that could support human life in an ethical way. He got it. He bought it. He reveled in it. If everyone had lived like he and his family did, raising their own food and hunting, there would never have been a problem.

Mr. Cruz's speech ended and the audience clapped again. The lights switched on, sunlight bounced in and filled the room. Waitstaff in white appeared pushing carts; some placed plates and silverware in front of the cadets while others placed dishes of food along the middles of the tables. Mr. Cruz explained they were eating farmed trout, a variety of lettuces and other raw vegetables grown at the camp, and amaranth flatbread. Filtered and oxygenated water was offered along with tea. Fresh lemons were given to everyone. A woman joined Mr. Cruz at the podium, and together they said grace, thanking those who prepared the meal, the creatures and plants that sacrificed themselves, plus the people who tended them, and the earth.

When Wesley looked up from the prayer, Grafton blew out a stream of hot air. "This is going to be a long two years," he said.

"What a diatribe of socialization," the redhead agreed. "What the hell is this anyway?" She asked, poking a forkful of trout to place it on her plate.

"Fish raised in environmentally controlled ponds full of chemicals, darling," Grafton responded.

"Don't forget the main ingredient–filtered water the fish swim in," added Wesley, regretting he was involved in such a conversation. "It's not like they're genetically modified fish," he added.

"I've never eaten fish before," the girl said, dryly. "Where I'm from, we continuously hear how bad fish is for you, how it's full of pollutants. They make it sound like the only fish alive are glowing with toxins." She tentatively stuck a bit in her mouth and made a face indicating distaste.

"They've been farming fish for hundreds of years, though it's really taken off since the turn of the century. It's called aquaculture. A lot of fish would probably be extinct now if we hadn't of figured out how to remove heavy metals and other toxins from ponds and tanks." Wesley tried some of the trout, too. Wary, he wished he had kept quiet. He hated sounding like a know-it-all.

Grafton pointed a fork Wesley's way. "Sounds like you've already been indoctrinated, roomie."

"Ah," Wesley didn't know what to say. "I don't think it's indoctrination to know about things like aquaculture and hydroponics. My family tries to live sustainably." Wesley looked over at the redhead. "It doesn't mean I agree with every regulation the government hands down." She nodded. Her hair was like copper or bronze, especially where the sunlight caught it. Her eyes were see-through blue, like a sky without rain, like sky somewhere besides Indiana.

Grafton chuckled a bit, dismissing the tension. "Well, this trout tastes pretty good no matter what they did to it."

The redhead rolled her eyes. "They didn't do anything to it. Didn't you listen to this guy?" She pointed toward Wesley. "All they did was provide it with the right living conditions, unlike the Southwest where they're letting everything blow away." She stuffed salad in her mouth and looked around like she was the most bored human being on earth.

Wesley heard laughter down the table to his left, and wished he were sitting with the kids down there. Still, the redhead was intriguing. He decided he'd ask her name. "My name's Wesley. What's yours?"

Her eyes came back to him. "I'm Nora Evans, Wesley. I'm from the land of sand, and absolutely no aquaculture." Her words were flat and dull, but pointed at the same time.

"I'm Grafton," Grafton edged in. He shook Nora's hand, and Wesley noticed how hairy his arms were. "I didn't want to come either, darling, but I happen to live a few hours away in Thomasville, Georgia, so I didn't have a chance to run. Mom made me come." Nora just looked down.

"Not to mention it's a federal crime not to," added Wesley. Grafton narrowed his bushy eyebrows and turned away.

Nora continued to look down at the table. She might be pretty, but she was seriously lacking in warmth. He remembered Tess, whom he had a crush on for the last four years. She was so shy. The one time she said "thank you" to him for passing back math homework, he about fell over. He rode his bike past her house, daydreamed about her constantly, but talking to her was like talking to someone who couldn't speak. She wasn't conversational, and it somehow made him silent too. So, he held the idea of her close and kept quiet.

Well, there was Sarah, too, but that hardly counted; it lasted two weeks total. Arguing about the exact definition of "freedom" destroyed their love. He had argued freedom took work and self-responsibility to maintain. She argued freedom meant anyone could do anything they wished. It was short, contentious, but there was that night on her back porch. He might as well have been a teenage monk if it wasn't for that porch experience.

More laughter spilled from the other end of the table. Several girls and guys looked like they were having fun. Nora stood up, accidentally banging into the table. She pivoted and walked away. Grafton jumped up after her, spilling a fork to the floor. Though he couldn't hear them, Wesley saw Grafton grab her. She turned and seemed to spit words out straight at him. She pulled away and stalked off. Grafton headed for the bathrooms, and Wesley ate another bite of farmed fresh trout. Clasping his hands under the table in prayer, he imagined soothing her with white light.

~»

After most plates had been retrieved by the waitstaff, many of the cadets wandered around the building or outside into the gardens and greenhouse. Grafton had come back to sit, but Nora had not. Wesley finished his fruit, texted Corey and Adam, and decided he'd walk around. The pressure of finding something to talk to Grafton about was worse than the pressure of saving the world.

He found himself in the gardens surrounded by a fountain and tall plants with thin, variegated leaves, and smaller, blooming plants decked out in pink, yellow, and blue. The air was hot and humid. There were cadets here and there, but they had mostly wandered back near the building. As he hopped from one stepping stone to the next, he came around a corner and saw

Nora. She looked tired and grumpy, like some kind of prickly plant. Wesley was afraid to approach her.

"I won't bite," she snapped.

Wesley took the opposite phrase. "I didn't think you would." He stood.

She stood. She sighed. She sighed again. "I guess we're stuck here for a while aren't we?"

He shook his head, afraid to say the wrong thing. What was the right thing? Everyone always said, "Just be yourself," which always seemed to be telling someone to be unique, do something wacky. So, he turned on his right heel, picked the closest flower, handed it to her, and bowed.

Her face lit up with a smile as delicate and strong as the ambiguity emanating off of her.

"Isn't it funny that here in this state, where they've suffered so much damage from climate change, the climate is somewhat stable, stable enough to grow flowers and fruit and plants?" He smiled, pointing at the yellow flower. "I believe it's a primrose willow." He smiled. "Our house has a few books on plants."

"I read books on mechanical engineering in my spare time," she quipped back.

"Really?" He hated that he just questioned her. Why did he do that?

"No, I really don't," she said, smiling again. "I'm not smart. I have more like, what would you call them, cowgirl skills."

"Real—" Wesley caught himself. "Cowgirl skills? That sounds interesting."

She seemed to suddenly withdraw into herself again. "They're obsolete skills. You know, herding cattle, killing wolves and big cats, living off the land."

Wesley looked around like he was going to tell her a secret. He wanted to see her smile one more time. "Living off the land is a very important skill in this new America we're rebuilding," he said. "It's up to us to fix what's broken." He tried his best to sound earnest. "Your skill set sounds appropriate for our new vision."

She guffawed, disgustedly. "That carbon-waste moron was right. You're already indoctrinated." She handed him the flower and walked away.

"I said the wrong thing," Wesley said aloud to no one.

COLIN WATERMAN

United Kingdom

Colin Waterman came to creative writing relatively late in life, after a successful career as an engineer.

He was curious whether the design and problem-solving skills he had honed in engineering would apply to creative writing (for example: working with the patterns and formulae of poetry), and he found that to some extent they did. But he concluded the key to success was to find a rule and break it. Waterman has had poems accepted for publication in The Stare's Nest and *Obsessed with Pipework.'* An account of his travels in Tibet appeared in *Real Travel* magazine. His science fiction novel *The Hesperian Dilemma* tackles the urgent theme of where technology is taking us, and if it adds to the growing pressure for mankind to find a sustainable way forward, then Waterman will consider his job done.

THE HESPERIAN DILEMMA

a novel excerpt

It is year 2134. The countries of the earth are polarised into two rival blocs, the Hesperian Federation in the west and the Khitan Empire in the east. The Hesperian military wing in space, known as OPDEO, has established a military base on Jupiter's second moon, Europa. Dr. Maura O'Hara has accepted a job to work there as an oceanographer. Accompanied by Geoff Kirby, a consultant for the Unified Nations, she is about to dive to the bottom of the ocean under the crust of ice. Just to find extremophile microbes would be sensational, as it would prove there is extraterrestrial life.

~»

Geoff agreed to dive with Maura. He downloaded the hazard analysis for bathyscaphe dives onto his com-pad, but quickly closed the page without reading it. He had to go diving, regardless of the danger. He boarded the maglev 'cage' and dropped down the two-kilometre-long vertical shaft through the ice. A member of dockside service personnel helped him change into a thermal suit and led him to the air lock. Geoff squeezed down the vessel's entrance tunnel to the observation gondola. He stepped into the cramped space too quickly and banged his head on an overhead valve. He thought Maura was about to laugh, but then he realised her smile was one of sympathy. He squatted down, hunched on the spare seat. She continued to fill in data records, relaying information to the support crew at Port Authority Control.

The basic design of a deep-sea bathyscaphe hadn't changed in two centuries. The main part of the vessel was a streamlined tube containing tanks for buoyancy and hoppers for ballast, and the gondola was a thick-walled steel sphere slung underneath. The internal diameter was no more than two metres, and the only place where Geoff could stand upright was in the centre. Maura, being petite and agile, had no difficultly moving around the cabin.

"Just waiting for clearance to dive," Maura told him. "Prof made me plan the temperature surveys myself, so I thought we'd start with the Cronus Rift. It's not deep by Europan standards, only 10,000 metres, but there's some volcanic activity on the seabed that causes local heating."

"Could there be some sulphur-eating microbes, by any chance?" said Geoff, trying to sound more nonchalant than he felt.

"There could be, right enough. But it would be grand just to find an amino-acid."

Maura detached the magnetic hooks tethering the craft to the quayside, and the dive began. Geoff felt more relaxed now they'd set off. Maura would have to pilot the craft manually as there were insufficient data on currents and other hazards for her to use auto-control. He realized this was an advantage for him, as he perched on his chair facing Maura, less than a metre away. She was oblivious to his gaze while he watched her frowning and pursing her lips as she made course corrections.

Cybernetics was one of Geoff's specialisms. He was fascinated by the way she scanned the screens and operated the controls. But he also studied her face, in frank appreciation of her perfect complexion, green eyes, and long, curly hair–deep chestnut-brown and parted in the middle. He felt certain her youth was genuine and, like him, she had never resorted to the regenerative drugs that were commonly used to reverse the effects of aging. His own self-denial had left him, aged thirty-five, with a pepper-and-salt hair colour and a beard to match. He wondered what her age would be. No more than mid-twenties?

Maura had been reporting to base at fifteen-minute intervals, but the port controller's voice was becoming increasingly distorted, the deeper they dived.

"Why is the line so bad?" asked Geoff.

"We have to use acoustic signals to communicate," Maura explained. "No one has found a way of using radio signals in deep water."

"It seems to be getting worse."

"We're getting close to the volcanic activity on the seabed. It's drowning the signal."

Geoff gave her a 'wouldn't you just know it' smile. He could feel the vibration through the walls of the gondola. It was as if the whole cabin was trembling. But what with, excitement? Or something else?

"Are you sure you want to carry on?" asked Maura. "If we go any deeper, we'll be on our own."

Geoff had known the Cronus Rift would be dangerous before they began the dive. He'd look like a coward if he backed out now. "It's okay," he said. "Let's have a quick look around and then get back up."

"Right then, get ready with the camera and shoot anything that looks interesting."

Geoff turned on the lights and peered out the observation window. "Wow!" he said in amazement. "It's like a scene from the Industrial Revolution. I can see hundreds of chimneys belching black smoke."

"Sure, they're on Earth's seabed too, you know."

"Really?" Geoff felt he should have done more research.

"It happens whenever hot water from geothermal springs erupts into the cold sea. The sulphides deposit out, making black smoke, and the buildup of minerals at the blowholes creates hollow towers." Geoff lifted his eyebrows, but made no comment.

They drove over vast fields of 'black smokers' and reached an area where many of the chimneys had fallen in random piles. "What's happened here?" Geoff asked. "Did they get too high?"

"We're on a fault line in the crust's tectonic plates. I think a seismic tremor brought them down."

"I'm panning with the camera. There's a piece of debris that seems to be moving around."

"Jaysis," said Maura. "We've hit the feckin' jackpot. There's something alive down there. I'll try to steer between the chimneys and get in close."

A violent jolt threw Maura and Geoff across the cabin and an ear-rending crash reverberated through the structure of the bathyscaphe. The vessel had stopped and was now tilting down at thirty degrees.

"Feckin' hell, I'll check for damage!" Maura scanned the alarms on the viz-box. "Forward buoyancy tank pressure: zero. For'ard water tank: zero. Port-side transverse propeller: kaput. Both bow floodlights are dead. Try the infrared camera."

"There's a chimney right across the bows," said Geoff. "Can we go backwards?"

"Aft propeller on full power now. Still stuck fast. I'm dumping the for'ard ballast. Nope, no change. I could ditch the aft ballast. The risk is we'll be out of control when we surface. We'll smack into the ice cap like a champagne cork. Shall I try it?"

"Just do it. We've got to get off the seabed somehow."

"Okay, I've opened the aft ballast hopper. We're about as light as we can be, but we're still not going anywhere."

"Can we call for help?" Geoff asked, trying hard to keep his voice steady.

Maura switched on the acoustic modem and a sound like a rocket exhaust filled the tiny cabin. She turned off the receiver. "Any other ideas?"

After an hour of trying to free their craft from under the stone cylinder, Geoff and Maura were strangely quiet. Geoff knew ranting and raving about their fate would only use their remaining oxygen more quickly. Even so, he felt strangely composed. *Am I in denial? Or is it that I don't want Maura to think I'm weak? Is my desire to seem calm and controlled greater than my urge to panic?*

All the sensory inputs to Geoff's brain had become more intense. The lights were brighter, and every creak of the damaged superstructure was amplified a thousandfold. Ignoring his emotions, Geoff's analytical brain began to break down the smell of the gondola into its separate components: the grease on the mechanical linkages, the electrolyte used in the ultra-capacitors, the tang of his own perspiration.

Once again, he studied Maura's face. Her lips were pressed tightly together, her eyebrows were lowered, and she was glaring at the flashing alarms on the viz-box screen. *What's she feeling? It won't help if she panics. But she's not showing signs of fear. Her body language means something else.*

"You're angry," he said.

"You bet I feckin' am!" said Maura. She balled her fists and looked around as if she wanted something to punch. She settled for thumping the control desk and then kicking it.

They stayed silent for a while. "D'you know why I'm fuming?" said Maura. "It's that feckin' fish."

"Er, sorry?"

"The fish—for the first time ever in the history of mankind, we found extraterrestrial life. And now it'll stay a secret."

"Someone will find it again, one day."

"If mankind doesn't destroy itself first!" Maura looked hard at Geoff. "You must regret coming with me. The only reason you're here is because you wanted to help." She shook her head. "I suppose I may as well tell you now. I think we would have been good together."

Thanks Maura, but this isn't a good time. But I'm glad she's talking. It'll calm her down and give me more time to think.

"Aren't you seeing anyone, Maura?" said Geoff, while scouring his brain for ideas of how to escape. *If we throw our weight from side to side, could we shake off the cylinder?*

"Not really," said Maura, smiling sadly. "There's been no one I wasn't happy to leave a billion kilometres away. All my relationships have been disasters."

"Why didn't they work out?" said Geoff. *Would we float if we detached the gondola and left the main hull behind?*

"Oh, there were lots of reasons. Some men wanted to lord it over me, and I wasn't having any of that. Some accused me of trying to dominate them, which I never did, not at all. But they all seemed to want me for their own benefit."

"Of course they did," said Geoff. "You'd be a benefit to anyone." *If we discharged our compressed air into the sea, would that shake us loose?*

"I don't mean in a good way," said Maura. "They wanted me just to hang on their arm, or make small talk to people they were sucking up to. I hated feeling I was being used!"

"So, none of them really cared about you?" said Geoff. *Keep thinking. There must be a way.*

"The bastards I met were so selfish!" said Maura. "They would have been crap fathers, I know that much." *She's getting angry again. I'll ask her about her work.*

"I thought you were a career scientist," said Geoff.

"I wanted to use science to help endangered species," said Maura. "How about you? What's your story, Geoff?"

"Oh, I got married young, too young," said Geoff, his train of thought interrupted.

Suddenly a clanking sound resonated through the vessel, and he felt the cabin levelling out. Maura was thrown out of her seat as the 'bath' lurched level again.

Geoff stooped to help her, but froze as he saw a shape on the viz-box screen, a shadowy, but familiar outline.

"Something's moved the chimney," he said, staccato tapping his viz-box screen to get the picture back.

Maura jumped up and began rapidly paging though the instrument readings. "We're going back up, thank God. What did you see on your screen?"

"I dunno. It's gone blank. We've lost the infrared."

"Something must have happened. Did the chimney just roll off?"

"Yeah, it must have done. P'raps it was a seismic tremor."

"You saw something. What was it?"

"Nothing, a hallucination, my blood oxygen's low."

"Tell me, Geoff. Something happened."

"I don't know. I thought there could be something there. It was just for a second. It'll be gone by now—if there was anything."

He checked the panel alarms. The forward searchlights had failed but the camera indicated its flash was still working. He operated the shutter. "Hey, Maura, look! What do you make of that? That thing—it looks like a crab, doesn't it?"

"Jaysis! I think I must have died already. I don't understand anything anymore, not at all."

"You've got it now, Maura. Evidence of extraterrestrial life. It's what you came here for!"

"Mary, Mother of God, it must be gigantic! It's taking us back up. And look at the depth readout. At this rate we'll be under the ice again in an hour."

"We could hit it hard. D'you want to contact Control? Say we're coming in for an emergency landing?"

She lifted a flap on the desk, and hit a button. "Okay, we're sending a Mayday, but no way am I opening the voice channel. I don't want to tell anyone we're being rescued by a crab."

"Look, I've got another photo," said Geoff. "It's not a crab, it's a machine. It's got a grab-arm and a rocket nozzle."

The crab machine accompanied the bathyscaphe all the way to the ice cap, retracing the course of their descent from Port Authority quayside. During the final fifteen minutes, Geoff had noticed their rate of ascent reduced, as if the machine was slowing them to minimise their impact with the ice cap.

"Glory be!" said Maura. "We're back at quayside. Where's the machine?"

"It seems to have disappeared. I could only see it now and again using the flash. It's probably dived back where it came from."

"I think we've got enough maneuverability to dock without help. But what in the universe was that thing?"

"It looked very mechanical to me. I think it was a robot."

"Whatever it was, something intelligent must have made it," said Maura.

She clutched her head with both hands and Geoff gripped her wrists to steady her. "Listen, please," he said, "the crab robot–promise me you'll keep it secret for the moment. There's something I haven't told you."

~»

Maura had agreed to meet Geoff in the Unidome sky-gallery. It was late morning Central Hesperian Time, but the blackness of the sky had an intensity unknown on Earth. Saturn floated high, the bands on its surface and gaps in its rings clearly visible. Geoff pointed out Titan and four of the planet's other moons, strung out like beads on a wire drilled through Saturn's equator. But his conversation sounded false even to his own ears. Their recent experience on the seabed weighed heavily on him. He knew he needed time to digest the significance of what had happened, both to them, and between them. For long minutes Geoff and Maura said nothing until, eventually, he asked how she was feeling.

"Actually I'm zinging, like you do if you breathe too much oxygen."

"Well, that sounds better than too little," said Geoff, the memory of their recent experience fresh in his mind. "But, tell me, did you see Prof? What happened?"

"Huh, it was funny. Would you believe he congratulated me? He praised me for what he thought was my skill in saving the bathyscaphe after it was damaged."

"Good for you," said Geoff. "You deserve Prof's praise after being so brave."

"Thanks. Prof was such a gobshite previously, I decided to take all the credit myself, at least for the time being. I mentioned you in dispatches though."

"So you didn't say anything about the crab robot?"

"I decided not to mention the crab-bot until after I'd talked to you. But really, we've got to tell everyone. It's feckin' cataclysmic!"

"That's why we've got to tread cautiously. We haven't got enough evidence yet," said Geoff.

"We've got photos of that crab-bot thing. It was made by some intelligent being. It's the most brilliantly wonderful news since Adam said 'Hiya' to Eve."

"No, we can't tell anyone. We have to find the robot-masters first." Geoff touched Maura's arm. She was a young woman who believed she'd made a supremely important scientific discovery, and he had to persuade her to keep it secret. "The Federation is desperate to achieve military superiority. They only want this place as a weapons base, and they won't allow anything to jeopardise it. When they find out another life-form exists in the sea, they'll try and destroy it."

"But we can show everyone what we've seen," said Maura. "OPDEO won't dare annihilate a new, intelligent species."

"Publishing some blurry pictures of a machine won't be enough to protect its makers. No matter what we say, OPDEO will claim it was their own robot that saved us. It's up to us to prove the aliens themselves exist. Until we've done that, we must keep what happened secret, okay?"

"Are you sure about all this? You're not paranoid, are you?"

"You don't know the half of it. The UN has been watching OPDEO for some time. There's no doubt they're utterly ruthless."

Geoff waited for Maura's reaction. Rhea, Saturn's second-largest moon, appeared from behind the planet, but still she remained silent, her lips pressed tight. Then at last she spoke. "Just before we docked, you said there was something you hadn't told me."

"Yeah, okay, I guess I'll have to come clean. For some time now, even before anyone landed here, the UN thought there could be life on Europa."

"Sure, that's not news. Everyone knows life could have started here."

"Well, not only did it start, it came a long way. In fact, it's come so far it can send messages across space."

"Jaysis! Are you coddin' me?"

"No, at least, not if you mean what I think you mean. Over a long period, the UN has received signals we've traced back to Europa."

"What sort of signals?" asked Maura, tilting her head to one side.

"We discovered strings of words written directly into our computer memories. We think it's only ever happened on our network."

"Why your computers?"

"Perhaps it was because the name of our subcommittee has 'peaceful' in it. At least, that's what I hope."

"Okay, what were the signals like?"

"The early ones were just gobbledygook. They looked like software errors. Then we went through a phase when we thought it was hackers having a bit of fun. Our internet security is the best in the world but, whatever firewalls we put up, somebody or something cut through them, like a thermite lance slicing a ship's hull."

"Very nautical, Geoff. But what was in the message?"

"It was a sort of flowery English, almost like poetry. We were convinced for a long time it was a hoax."

"Come on, for Chrissakes, tell me what the messages said."

"It's not that easy to say. I think an extraterrestrial was trying to work out how to communicate with us. Now we've had our lives saved by the crab-bot, I'm certain the messages were an attempt to contact us. Some living being was looking for peaceful acceptance and a mutually beneficial relationship."

"You mean it wanted to be friends?"

"You could say that."

"D'you think the crab-bot sent the messages?"

"I don't think so. My guess is it was being manipulated by something else, either from inside or outside. Thanks to you, I've now got strong evidence that advanced aliens live on this moon, just as the UN suspected. I will write them a coded report."

Maura looked pensive. Then she broke away from Geoff and stood with her hands on her hips. "So now I know your game. You've been cosying up to me so you could go looking for aliens."

"Hey, that's not fair," said Geoff, thinking hard. *Maura isn't being rational. If I explain, she'll understand we've been sharing a common interest.*

"Hang on," he said. "You asked me to help you search for living organisms. I was more than willing to, because I was on the same search. The only difference was I expected my organisms to have a higher IQ than yours."

"Now you're just being a smart-arse." Maura smeared away a tear from her cheek.

Geoff was confused. *What have I missed? What I said was entirely logical, wasn't it? I've done something wrong and it's made her unhappy.*

"Why are you upset?" he asked. 'I don't understand. You were a real hero when we were trapped on the seabed."

"Let me alone, I'll talk to you tomorrow," and she walked off leaving Geoff staring at the icy landscape.

~»

General Flannery returned Major Breckenridge's salute. He walked over to a drinks cabinet in the corner of his office, half-filled two glasses with Bourbon, and poured in ice until the liquid was just short of the rim. "I heard you were good at baseball, Major. We ought to start a team. How about the OPDEO Strikers? I've been reading your report. You certainly gave that fucker what for."

"Thank you, suh," said Breckenridge, his face momentarily contorted by a nervous tic. "I love them supercavitation torpedoes. They fly like rockets. The insurgent never knew what hit it." He downed his whiskey in one gulp and the general gave him another.

Flannery shifted his overflowing in-tray and sat on the edge of his desk. "It was a smart move defusin' the explosive. You disabled the machine without wreckin' it. What's the latest analysis?"

"Well it was definitely unmanned, suh, or what the heck you call the critters that built it. Nothin' was livin' inside. It was made from some real fancy alloys, and it had steam jets for propulsion. It used a lotta technology we've never seen before."

"What was its purpose? Was it military?"

"I don't think so. It had a hell of a big claw, and a lot of cuttin' gear. We think it was designed for maintenance, suh."

"So, what d'you think controlled it, Major?"

"It had a lot of complicated control programs. We know that from the chips we've found, pico-arrays with awesome memories. Our geeks are checkin' 'em out right now, suh." The major's face was looking flushed, and his habitual tic had reduced to a flicker of his eyelid.

"Was it autonomous, Major? A slave drone? Or could it make decisions?"

"Aw, we're workin' on that right now, suh. One of the chips looks like a receiver for external commands. We're scannin' the ocean for acoustic signals. That's how we think the machine gets its orders."

"So, you reckon our oceanographers discovered the machine before us, but never told us about it?"

"It certainly looks that way. O'Hara and Kirby say they got their bathyscaphe stuck under some rocks on the seabed. But it was never just a rock that caused damage like that on the hull."

"How d'you mean?"

"I raced a lotta stock cars in my youth, suh. Smashed 'em up and welded the good halves together. For me it's a lead-pipe cinch, that vessel's been gripped by mechanical jaws and the debris cut away with a torch. Shall I bring 'em in for questionin', suh?"

"No, not yet. I think we can use 'em to find out more, at their risk." Flannery sat back, steepling his fingers. "O'Hara clearly wasn't tellin' us the truth. If they've had contact with aliens, they'll try it again, and I wanna see what happens."

~»

Geoff was desperate to talk to Maura. He called and arranged to meet her in the Unidome garden. She was sitting on a park bench, watching tiny hummingbirds hovering over a scarlet *Etlingera* flower. It was lunchtime, and groups of two or three people wandered around, relaxing before going back to work. Geoff felt the garden turning around him as the combined scents of hibiscus, frangipani, and white champak saturated his senses. He caught hold of the armrest and dropped into the empty space on the bench.

"Maura, we need to talk. You said I'd been cosying up to you to hitch a free ride under the ice. And yes, that was true in a way. I admit I had an ulterior motive, but it wasn't the only reason I wanted to get to know you." Geoff blurted his words in a rapid staccato. He failed to notice Maura begin to smile and then compose her face to look serious again.

"I would have told you earlier why I was sent here," he continued, "but I was afraid you'd think I was crazy." He put his arm around her shoulder, but Maura gently removed it.

"It's okay," she said. "I forgive you, but no hanky-panky, okay?

Actually, I need to talk to you. I think OPDEO suspects something."

"I don't think we've done anything to upset them, have we?" said Geoff. "Not yet, anyway."

"Well, the bathyscaphe went in for repairs and the technicians have been photographing the damage. They've found scorch marks from something like an oxyacetylene torch. And there are indentations that look like the hull was gripped by something powerful."

"Oh heck, d'you think they realise something helped us?"

"I don't know," said Maura. "But an OPDEO major has been crawling over the hull too. I had to see Prof yesterday. I thought he was going to give me the third degree about what happened on the seabed."

"Is he suspicious too?"

"Actually, he was as nice as pie. He wants me to go diving again in the spare 'bath' as soon as possible. He said he needed more temperature data from the Cronus Rift. He even told me to take you as my crew."

Geoff was relieved Maura was talking to him again. But there was something very odd about what she'd just said. He sat listening to the sound of a pair of hummingbirds, rising and falling in volume to a regular beat.

"You know," he said at last, "I think OPDEO already knows about the crab-bot. Earlier today, one of the OPDEO programmers asked me for advice on something he was working on. His boss had downloaded some hardware device and given him a printout of machine code."

"Why did he ask you?"

"He shouldn't have spoken to me, but he was under a lot of pressure. He knew I had a background in Artificial Intelligence and he asked me what the program was for."

"That's weird. Don't they have manuals for their software?"

"It wasn't OPDEO programming. In fact, it was in a code I'd never seen before, but it used highly developed back propagation routines."

"Sorry, that means absolutely nothing to me," said Maura with a dismissive wave.

"Well, what if I said there were subroutines for operating a jib with a grabbing device? What would that make you think of?"

"You mean like a crab-bot?"

"Exactly. I think OPDEO have captured our robot friend, or one of its kind. They're probably dissecting it to see what it's made of. If I'm right, OPDEO know there's extraterrestrial life in the ocean."

"So they know that we know. Is that it, Geoff? Perhaps they'll stop us diving again."

"Maybe, or they may have ordered Prof to send us back to the Cronus Rift, hoping the bots, or their masters, will contact us."

"Holy Mother of God, you mean now we have to go searching for extraterrestrials after our fellow humans have taken apart one of their robots?"

"Exactly," said Geoff. "OPDEO could use any encounter to learn more about the aliens, without putting themselves at risk."

"But, even if we meet the ETs, I don't understand how OPDEO will find out. There's no way they can see us in the Rift."

"They don't need to. They could bug the inside of the observation gondola. Then they'd rerun the recordings after we've come home again, assuming that we do come back. And if the aliens turn nasty, then we'll just be another tragic news item."

Maura sat looking at Geoff, her arms crossed. "So according to you, we've been set up. Up to our necks in the Wicklow bog and sinking fast. What are we going do now?"

"Well, I think we'd do best to stick to my plan. If we can get direct proof the aliens exist, then we can tell the world. That'll make it much harder for OPDEO to destroy a whole new biological domain."

"You're certain OPDEO are a load of heartless bastards? I thought they were ecologically friendly."

Geoff looked Maura full in the face. Somehow, he had to get the seriousness of the situation across to her. "I've seen secret UN reports," he said. "They show OPDEO plans a preemptive strike on the Khitan Empire on Earth. They don't care about human life, never mind aliens."

"Mother of God—if you're right, the aliens may not be so friendly next time we dive. Last time a crab-bot came to rescue us. It could just as easily have sawn us in two."

"True, and I cannot guess what might happen if we dive again. But I still have one trick up my sleeve. The UN gave me something, just in case I could ever leave a message."

"How do you know what language they speak–if they speak?"

"I don't know. But what I've got is a copy of one of those plaques carried by the *Pioneer* spacecraft in the early 1970s. You know, a diagram of the solar system with an arrow pointing to Earth, and fundamental data about hydrogen and stuff that extraterrestrials ought to recognise."

"With the picture of the naked man and woman? I always thought it would give aliens funny ideas."

"At least the man was waving–with his hand I mean–I'd better shut up." Geoff was relieved to see Maura had given up trying to look serious, and they both began to laugh.

"So, what you're saying is there are creatures we know nothing about and, unless we risk our lives again, they may not even make it to a natural history museum."

"We don't have to do any of this, Maura. But we're on the verge of a breakthrough that could change mankind. I'm prepared to take the risk, if you are."

"We'll be like two worms on a hook. When d'you want to go squirming?" Maura stood up and wriggled her hips. Geoff copied her, and they both collapsed back onto the bench, chortling happily.

DEVANSHI JACKSON

India & United States

Born in India, Devanshi Jackson was fifteen when her family immigrated to the US. She is an environmental engineer and a keen data scientist. Her passion for environmental preservation and biology-inspired innovations has spilled into many of her writings. Her love of literature began at a very young age; while listening to her parents sing Hindu hymns, she often felt the presence of great poets.

Though Jackson has written many poems, "Reasoner" is her first short story. The inspiration for "Reasoner" (which was an assignment for a creative-writing class at a local library) came while she was waiting for her daughter to finish soccer practice and witnessed a perfect ruby fall sunset beyond the woods!

REASONER

a short story

The leaves rustle at the base of the tree. It is just an animal skipping around, looking for nuts or creatures to eat. I live in an enormous tree with amazing views. My habitat has rewarded me with many fond memories, including swinging from a grapevine from a hundred feet above the ground and finding holes filled with rainwater in the side of the trunk where new life begins. But it is a monumental task to reach the top section of my tree house when I desire to bask in the sun. The tree is alive on the inside; it keeps me warm, the sap and nuts feed me all year long.

It is a warm summer day and I leave to make a long journey to the next wood to meet with a beloved friend–Violet. We take turns once a year to visit each other; though we would like to meet more often, the spring is too wet, winter is too cold, and fall is a busy time collecting food for winter. I have known Violet for a long time, since the days of schooling at the Vidyapith of Biomimicry. It is common for the wood-dwelling humans to live well beyond the age of one hundred years. In the first century we acquire knowledge, establish habitat, and develop great friendships. After our one hundredth birthday celebration many of us choose to retire to the Vidyapith to teach, but some of us remain independent researchers, doing field studies, observing and analyzing trends that impact our planet. Violet is turning 115 today! She has mastered the art of harnessing energy from the sun—photosynthesis, even after her tree has lost all its leaves. As I near her wood I am filled with excitement and can hardly wait to tell Violet about my invention of PhotoAqua pump that uses the tree root system in the winter to obtain water. The best part is that the pump uses Violet's invention of photosynthesis energy generator.

My walking speed gets faster, and I'm feeling unusually warm and blinded by streaming sunlight. Suddenly the tree canopy has disappeared, the branches are leafless, and trees are warping. Some of the trees have lost big limbs; the wood looks very dry. I run to Violet's tree home with my heart pounding, vision sharpened, and thoughts racing. My only wish is to find Violet. Violet's tree is still standing tall but the bark has no woody summer smell. No ferns are growing at the base of her home; there is no sign of intrusion or exit. I think back to the weather events of the past year, but my memory is blurred. I can't even decide if I feel Violet's presence. We wood-dwelling humans have highly developed senses and believe in letting the nature take the course. Being a human has left me with overwhelming emotions, drowning my astute ability to reason!

ELIZABETH ESGUERRA CASTILLO

Philippines

Born in Manila, Philippines, Elizabeth Esguerra Castillo is a professional feature writer, journalist, travel writer, award-winning poet and author, editor, proofreader, and speaker.

Castillo is the author of *Seasons of Emotions* (UK) and *Inner Reflections of the Muse* (USA). Her international recognitions include 2nd Place for "Poet of the Year, 2013" in an international poetry contest of Destiny to Write Publications in the UK with her first international poetry book, *Seasons of Emotions,* in 2nd Place for "Book of the Year, 2013". *Winning Strategies Magazine* also awarded her the "Over-all Winner in the Winning Strategies International Winners Award" for her positive influence in her community and around the world in 2013, and she won an "Inspirational Poet" award at the PENTASI B World Friendship Poetry Celebration and Historical Forum held at the National Museum of the Philippines that same year. She is also a consistent Highly Commended Faith-Centered Poet at the International Community of Poets (ICOP), Destiny Poets based in the United Kingdom.

Castillo's articles and poems have also appeared in international online magazines and literary magazines. She has co-authored more than sixty poetry anthologies in the US, UK, Canada,

Romania, Africa, and India, including *Live Life: The Daydreamer's Journal,* a global charity anthology for the benefit of the American Cancer Society released in 2012 and a world-record holder for the most number of artists contributing to an anthology.

Castillo is a member of the American Author's Association (AAA), Asia Pacific Writers & Translators (APWT), PEN International, and World Association of Authors and Researchers (WAOAR) as well as a contributing editor for *Inner Child the Magazine* (USA), and an advisory board member of *Reflection Magazine,* an international literary magazine.

TAKE ME BACK TO GENESIS

Existence of humankind came to be in the Garden of Eden,
Lush greeneries abound as the Almighty created a bountiful haven
From darkness, He illuminated the Earth with fruit-bearing trees for
His special creations,
There was no famine nor lack of natural resources to be able to live a
decent life here in this world
The Tree of Life in the middle of Adam and Eve's heaven, the Eternal
Source of youth and innocence.

Trees are our friends, the ones who stood by us during floods and hunger,
Can you see now the devastation of the mountain ranges and of barren
forests and jungles?
Oh, won't you take me back to the age of Genesis when there is still
Eternal Life and bliss,
Take me back to the time when hugging a tree puts your soul in peaceful serenity
Yes, I wish to get back in time when everywhere I lay my eyes on around me, lovely trees enliven my weary soul.

Take me back to Genesis when all beautiful creations live harmoniously in their natural habitat,
The time when the Earth was not plagued with natural disasters of all sorts
When natural calamities such as strong hurricanes seem not to curse
the land and take away lives,
Take me back to Genesis when all is well, there is unity and camaraderie and love dwells in most hearts.

Oftentimes we ask Mother Nature why so much devastation is witnessed
in present times,
But do we also question ourselves what did we do to destroy the environment and later suffer the consequences?
At the beginning of time, there were no deadly disasters leaving us
homeless and hopeless,
We need to awaken and be responsible for every deed, be enlightened
that Mother Nature is teaching us valuable things
Would you go back to Genesis when every living thing is taken care of
and protected in the Garden of Eden?

EYES WITHOUT A FACE

I suddenly jumped out of a mysterious lingering dream that seems to be haunting
But didn't quite leave me out screaming,
A wandering eye scans the vast space in time reflecting with a weary
stare quite saddening.
Through this crystalline mirror I witnessed how the world came to be
How it was created by the invisible hand of our loving Almighty
Out of love He gave life to things that are meant to be magnificent, stunning and carefree,
That's the genesis of it all but look at how terror in this once peaceful paradise now reign
People inflicting each other incessant pain,
What happened to this once beautiful Earth His masterpiece?
Can we ever find harmony and eternal bliss?

These eyes without a face out of the blue started to weep
As slideshows of evil doings of mankind flashed before my very naked eyes,
I suddenly felt pain piercing from a deep part of me
But what can I do alone amidst all these misery?
Mercy for me and my brethren came overflowing this heart of mine
Staring at these teary eyes I begin to question myself

Have I done my fellowmen good?
Although different predicaments were not at times fully understood
Have I fed the hungry, offered shelter to the homeless, listened to a
weary lost soul?
And be a friend to someone who feels alone amongst crowds of hypocrite people.

A beaming light then blurred these eyes without a face
As an angel stepped down from a heavenly pedestal lead me to a room
With immaculate white walls and shiny crystal ball at the center of
this sanctuary
I was asked to take a peek at what our Earth used to be covered with greeneries,
Clear, blue skies and all are in dire harmony.
No drought, no deadly floods claiming innocent lives at a snap
No bombings, no power struggle for supremacy, everything was so simple then
But as man acquired advanced knowledge and skills
He became self-centered, rude and discontent,
We are our brother's keeper and Mother Earth is our responsibility
Not just a refuge, a shelter but the heaven's gift to mankind.

MAIA KUMARI GILMAN

Canada & United States

A writer, Architect, artist, and Reiki Master whose award-winning work has been featured by USA Today and the Sundance Channel, Maia Kumari Gilman grew up in Canada and now lives in the United States in New Jersey with her husband and their two children. Gilman is the author of the eco-fiction novel *The Erenwine Agenda* (ASEI Arts, 2017) and is currently writing her next novel, *Otter Coast,* which has a focus on creative states of consciousness. A third and related novel-in-the-works, *Rail,* touches on the complexities of high-speed transport in the modern world.

Gilman has published numerous nonfiction green building articles, and contributed a case study to *How to Design and Build a Green Office Building: A Complete Guide to Making Your New Or Existing Building Environmentally Healthy* (Atlantic Publishing Company, 2011).

As visual artist, Gilman expresses herself not only through the written word, but also through color and line. In 2018 she showed her work in the group exhibition Domus Terrae, an art show held at the United Nations in Geneva, Switzerland, to honor the international negotiations of the UN around migration and refugees. She exhibits her work locally in the New York area and maintains a private art studio in New Jersey.

BIOREME

a short story

Annabelle Walkerton took a last look at herself in the dim bathroom and spoke aloud to the reflection in the mirror. "You can do this. It'll be worth it." The ever-present knot in her belly had released enough so that her breath fell in sync with the subtle pulse offered by the Bioreme up the street. So close, and yet she'd never been. It was time, wasn't it? She'd never seen herself as a shut-in, but when the knot of anxiety in her belly had become so great, she'd found herself paralyzed to go out. Now, though, something bigger clicked inside her in rhythm with an outer pull, and she responded to its call. She picked up the brooch from atop her dresser, where she'd kept it all these years. Put it on? No, she pocketed it. Just in case.

The ritual of getting to the Bioreme many times in one day would have been too much for her, and only the most hardcore devotees of the process–employees of the town who maintained it–were seen there around the clock. What a nice benefit for those workers, to be paid to be in a Bioreme. And yet, she didn't have to pay to go in–it was free to her, anytime, every day.

Payment or nonpayment wasn't the issue for her—the thought of getting out of the house was the larger thorn.

The front doorknob of her tidy house closed heavy in her hand, she on the outside of it, looking at the garden she'd turned over to the town for vegetables, and up the street, now clear of vehicles. She'd been told it hadn't always been that way, free of private cars. The ChargeCars station was near but she hadn't visited, in spite of its easy access and the service's offer to pick her up to bring her to it.

Like the Bioreme. Such easy access and she'd not taken advantage of it—she supposed it had been up to her all that time, all that time she'd been waiting for someone or something to urge her up and out of the house. Conveniences made it so easy to stay in: groceries delivered; food picked from her front yard by the town and put inside; all her finances handled remotely, from within the walls of her own home. She barely remembered what it was to visit a bank, something she'd not done in decades. Life's choices, the full array of them, made it so easy to follow any path, really. She no longer wanted the interior-feeling, anxious knot path she'd been on.

It didn't matter what triggered the change in her, and she didn't owe anyone an explanation. It was time; that was all. Annabelle felt a new rhythm. She turned away from her house, a nod to the chirpy birds around the vegetable garden, and looked toward the Bioreme up the street. She wondered where the lines ran, from her house up to the pod: Beneath the road, or under the plantings? She'd moved in after the Installation, hadn't seen them at work with the town retrofit of the water system.

A philanthropist, she'd heard. Just takes one. Her breath came in short bursts up the hill. Maybe she should have called the ride after all. *Walk, Walkerton!* They were all over now, these pods.

They'd come to the philanthropist in a dream and they were emerging like popcorn. Popping Bioremes! The image made her belly glow a warmth she'd not felt in a long time. The pods were multiplying as other regions caught on, saw the benefit in small-scale biofiltration.

She could see it closer, now. She began to notice the environment around her as she approached. It did not press upon her, and yet was inviting. It had been so long since she'd felt invited somewhere, and up for accepting the invitation. The knot in her belly, as little as it had become on the walk up, niggled at her as if to remind her, "you don't have to do this," but she continued. Others arrived as she did, some escorted, some on wheels, some carried. It was not a crowded time, this mid-morning she'd chosen. A handful. She'd miss the blue light, but no matter. A school group was leaving and she stepped aside for the kids in their snakelike line, weaving back out to their school around the corner.

She gave her hand a wave at the entrance and she was scanned: "Annabelle Walkerton, cleared for entry," said the device. Her belly did a little flip. It would be ok. Didn't matter. Belly would settle. She took a deep breath. The air was a little humid, fresh smelling of reeds; the glowing dome of the Bioreme capped the microenvironment like a crown. The town employees on shift moved between the reed beds and the light pipes, and she found a bench that appeared to connect different growing zones. She sat, and exhaled.

If she'd wanted, she could have asked, but no one approached her. If she'd wanted, she could have read the signs, but she chose not to. She wanted to breathe in the goodness of this light-filled, plant-aware, sacred space she'd found right in the middle of her own neighborhood.

~»

Marina loved this old thing. Old, not really, she liked to think of it as old since it'd been there since she entered high school, and she was so old now, at twenty-four. And she'd begun to give her time there, to the Bioreme, at fourteen. Inspired on opening day to see what it was all about, way back then.

She'd liked the pipes. The reed beds. The filtration screens, and the swish-click-swish sound they made when they were being cleaned and changed. Don't clean 'em too hard, let the bacteria do its thing—that was the trick, she'd been told.

And for ten years–first as a volunteer and now as paid staff–that was her job: to manage the swish-click-swish changeover time at the Bioreme, at blue dawn and blue dusk, when she would whisper to each little bacterium, *Swim! Swim! Swim!* And the municipal water would receive its refreshment, just like that.

Marina thought it quite funny that chatting with bacteria at dawn and dusk should be a part of a job description–"encourager of biofiltration," it ought to be called. It wasn't, of course, but she liked to think of it that way.

Encourager of humans, now that was more like it. She nodded to them when they came in, alone or in groups, and she showed them the filtration beds if they asked, but only when they did. Those ones weren't there for a tour. They were there for the other thing–the thing she couldn't name, that happened at the blue light of dawn and the blue light of dusk–and in between. It was a mesmerizing thing to see, these humans coming one by one for their turning.

The turning was like a healing but it wasn't. There was nothing wrong with these people that they should need a healing. But a turning–yes. They turned themselves over in the Bioreme, and then they went out into the world, turned. Changed. Charged up. Integrated. No matter what falsities they arrived with, they left with their inner perfection apparent and radiant, a wholeness that made Marina wonder: What was this work at the Bioreme? Water filtration, biofiltration, for the subzone of the municipality in which she lived. And they were all over, since ten years ago, and still emerging, these Bioremes.

They employed people, they hydrated the town, purified its black and grey water–and these Bioremes, they turned people.

It was most amazing, thought Marina. Take this one here–that woman who'd come in. She was turning, Marina could see it. The woman sat alone on a bench between the big reed bed vats, and Marina could see her deep inhalation-exhalation even from the other side. A definite turner.

Marina's boss approached the sitting woman–the turner—and for a moment, Marina wondered if the woman would run away. The turner smiled–Marina could see it, the smile, from where she stood, under the high arc of the conservatory dome. The Bioreme bounced their voices up to the glass roof and back down to Marina, and she heard.

~»

Cameron saw her before she saw him. Would Annabelle be happy to see him? It had been years since–well, no matter. He felt her turn before she did it–and he knew she'd be smiling.

She turned.

~»

Marina saw the completion of the turn, and in that moment, she had words: it was the See Me As I Am, felt and projected from within the turner, for all to see, should they choose, and not, if they did not choose. And from that point forward, Marina understood the work of the Bioreme to be about so much more than filtration.

~»

Annabelle felt him before she saw him and knew him by the feeling of his approach. Even after all these years of avoidance (of him, of everyone, of the potential of him in everyone), diagnosis (agoraphobic) and distress (she could not conjure that, now, sitting in the Bioreme)–even after all that, she knew that feeling.

~»

Somebody died in the Bioreme. Not as dramatic as all it could have been, but still left a feeling Marina could not shed. Nobody drowned or slipped or got poisoned by the pretreatment wastewater, nothing like that. A simple heart-stopping moment for one life, and that life happened to choose the Bioreme as the place to shift.

Fine. Marina was the one who'd been given the task of following up at Civic Center with the Finalization. Finalization sounded so final, an echo of the past, almost as bad as Death Certificate. She'd been able to do it for her boss, Bioreme Director Casey, quickly, on her lunchtime–and why did she have to actually go to Civic Center when it could all be done remotely? That she never understood, but she didn't mind, because it seemed the respectful thing to do, to show up, especially since the transitioned one had no known family.

The building of Civic Center was an oldie, a big stone affront that went back, way back, over three hundred years. An old ramp up the side went unused and a Hover Lite had been installed over the steps. She was tempted to try it, but there was already someone in play there, so she took the stairs. Maybe on the way back down.

Inside, a creaky elevator took her to the top floor–of all the innovations of the time, could they not have replaced the elevator too? She'd have to ask. It even had the beautiful brass grate that she had to pull across, accordion style. At least the buttons had been upgraded to hand-scan.

"I'm here for the witnessing of the finalization of someone who transitioned in the Bioreme," she said into the monitor at the door, and nothing happened. "Finalization," she said, and the door opened once the scanner picked up her identity. A goybirl met her on the inside and led her through. "Why the old elevator? I was sure it would have been replaced along with the other mechanical stuff."

"Secretary of the Interior Standards–historic restoration. Couldn't shake it! Still waiting in Congress." The goybirl smiled and let Marina in through to the inner sanctum of the Civic Center's finalization space. "You're here for the Bioreme death. The cremation was done already and the ashes are boxed–do you want them?"

"Isn't it supposed to be a bit more formal than that? I thought I had to witness something–to be present for something."

The goybirl retrieved a case through a pneumatic tube arrangement. "They never upgraded this old mail system, either, but it's fun, useful for these." They handed a little metal box to Marina. "I don't know what you'll do with this, shake it into the Bioreme or in the woods. Whatever you do, don't let it near a Hover Lite or it'll make a huge mess."

"It's in a box."

"The Hover Lite doesn't care what's in a box or not. It moves in a stream, see–and the cheap metal of the box can flow. That's why no jewelry allowed."

"What if someone has metal in their body?"

"That's fine. It's the low-grade stuff that breaks down. They're working the kinks out of it. Don't you have one at the Bioreme?"

"No we're all on one level–all flat. Except for the going up high to get access to the conservatory dome, but they do that on rope ladders."

"Ropes! Are you serious? How archaic."

"We put in for an upgrade but we're waiting."

"Nothing magical about waiting."

"I should go." Marina waved the box in the air. "Thanks–for the finalization."

"The scanner will catch you on the way out. Lift the box."

"Kind of lonely here?"

"Naw, everyone's out on lunch at the stream."

"Not you?"

"You caught me."

"Glad I did, don't know how I would have done this without a human." Marina switched the box to her left and shook hands with the goybirl. "Marina."

"Ringga."

"That's a pretty name." Marina smiled and lifted the box. "Till the next time, Ringga."

"And there will always be a next time," said Ringga. "I wish they'd stop calling them finalizations. There's nothing final about it!"

"Come to the Bioreme sometime," Marina said. "I think you'd like it. A different side of civics. I'll tour you if you like." She'd been dying to tour someone but hadn't thought she had the ability–maybe she could show off her touring skills to Director Casey and put in for a new job. Enough whispering to bacteria at blue light. It all went on demonstration, and this might be her chance.

"I would like. And I will." Ringga opened the door for Marina and led her back out to the elevator. The creaky old elevator. "I'll hold the box if you like and you can use the Hover Lite over the stairs." Ringga came into the elevator and they went down together.

"Will this be ok?" Marina lifted the leg of her pants to reveal her peg leg. "I've never tried a Hover Lite with this."

"Can you pop it off? No, you should be fine. Tuck your pant leg into your sock and that should absorb the wave of it." Ringga held the metal box with the ashes while Marina leaned on the wall of the elevator and made her adjustments.

"Exciting! I never had a chance to do this. Everything's all on one level where I live and work." The elevator lurched to a quick stop and Marina accordion-creaked the brass gate into open. "You hang onto the box and take the stairs, yes? What would somebody do if they had to do this on their own?"

"They could do it, but the metal might degrade a bit on the box. My gran said it's like putting cheap plastic in a microwave."

"Aha. Yeah my gran has one of those too."

"Hey you know what my gran has at her place? A toaster—one of the really old ones that sit on a stove burner. She collects them." Ringga stood at the top of the stairs and held the little cremation box in their hands. "Ok you go now."

Marina stood at the top of the stairs, balanced, peg leg tucked in for safety. Hopefully the thing wouldn't glitch out on her. They were supposedly all over now, at least in the civic spaces. Not in the Bioreme, where they weren't needed.

"Speak it—what you want it to do. You can do it in your head too but it's usually doubly clear if you say it out loud."

"Take me downstairs?"

"It perceives doubt—it corrects for that in your voice inflection and neural frequencies."

"Take me downstairs!" She stepped up to the plate and closed her eyes. Felt the uplift—and the swoosh—and the downlighting—and the landing. "Wow, like an arc. I felt the arc!" She opened her eyes and saw she'd landed beautifully at the bottom of the staircase, where Ringga approached.

"You might be more sensitive because of the metal in your peg leg."

"It's mostly carbon sequestered polymer plastic."

"Oh that'll do it. The carbon. Where'd you get that, anyway? I thought those bios were all metal."

"I got it as a free trial on one of those carbon capture projects they had going a few years ago. You know the ones the Environmental Protection Agency sponsored before they changed their name to EIA?"

"Environmental Influence Agency."

"It's lasted pretty well. I like thinking I have a bit of atmosphere holding me up." Marina gave a chuckle. Took the box back from Ringga. "I don't understand how someone with a metal piece would use the Hover Lite–or someone in a standing chair? If you can't take metal in, how do you do that?"

"Oh those are all made of compatible metals. They figured out the galvanic action. It's the cheap jewelry that's more of a problem. High-vibration metals are fine."

"You want to come to the Bioreme now? Seems like you have a lunch break time too, yes? You can come and see a turner or two. There was a fun one this morning. Looked like a love story."

~»

Cameron Casey folded the tablet sheet into four and tucked it under his arm. Annabelle needed some more time in her turning, he knew, yet he felt agitated and impatient that she'd come all that way, and had not answered his pressing question. The tablet sheet pressed cold in his side and he clung to it for cool comfort. He headed back to the office at the periphery to put it back, his engineering roundup complete. Not complete—interrupted, by his visioning of Annabelle in the Bioreme. He'd have to get back to the municipal Monthly Check once his mind could return into its focus.

"Director Casey? I'm going to tour a visitor, can you come? I mean, please come while I tour this visitor." Marina cleared her throat and faced her companion. "Let's do this."

Cameron was caught unprepared. "Fine. Let's go back out." He shifted the tablet sheet to the other side and shook hands with the visitor. "Director Cameron Casey. Welcome." He'd be back out in Annabelle's sphere. And her answer hung heavy in the humidity of the space, waiting for him to grab onto it. He'd better get ready to line up with whatever it was she had to say.

The visitor led the way, pointing out vats and pipes, the ladders (ropes! they exclaimed), the metal grates underfoot. Marina answered every question and did not hesitate to provide overall explanation. A visitor-led exploration, as it should be. Marina was ready. He'd promote her to the next tier of management at the next Weekly.

It might take some pressure off. He could step back and let Marina lead. Maybe he did have energy for Annabelle's pace, after all. There was room for change, in all of them. All changing, all the time, not at the same rate, or with the same intention. Kind of like lining up bacterium one by one in the Bioreme–a seemingly impossible task, except when handled in one visualized sweep at blue light. Time for a change of management. Maybe he'd turn the whole thing over to Marina's care, and he and Annabelle could shift together, somewhere, here, elsewhere, he didn't know. Didn't care. Caught up to Marina and her visitor, gave her a nod. "I'll be on the other side. You're looking good, holler if you need me." He'd spotted Annabelle as she moved around the beds, and he wondered if he could ask again. Was there a statute of limitations on proposals of marriage?

www.ingramcontent.com/pod-product-compliance
Lightning Source LLC
Chambersburg PA
CBHW070428010526
44118CB00014B/1945